France since the Revolution

TEXTS AND CONTEXTS

Edited by Claire Gorrara and Rachael Langford

Cardiff University

A member of the Hodder Headline Group
LONDON
nited States of America by
y Press Inc., New York

First published in Great Britain in 2003 by
Arnold, a member of the Hodder Headline Group,
338 Euston Road, London NW1 3BH

http://www.arnoldpublishers.com

Distributed in the United States of America by
Oxford University Press Inc.,
198 Madison Avenue, New York, NY10016

The advice and information in this book are believed to be true and
accurate at the date of going to press, but neither the authors nor the publisher
can accept any legal responsibility or liability for any errors or omissions.

British Library Cataloguing in Publication Data
A catalogue record for this book is available from the British Library

Library of Congress Cataloging-in-Publication Data
A catalog record for this book is available from the Library of Congress

ISBN 0 340 76360 4 (hb)
ISBN 0 340 76361 2 (pb)

1 2 3 4 5 6 7 8 9 10

Typeset in 10/12½pt Sabon by Phoenix Photosetting, Chatham, Kent
Printed and bound in Great Britain by MPG Books Ltd, Bodmin, Cornwall

What do you think about this book? Or any other Arnold title?
Please send your comments to feedback.arnold@hodder.co.uk

Contents

List of contributors

Gordon Cumming is Lecturer in French at Cardiff University. He teaches on colonial and post-colonial relations with Africa and researches widely on French and British development policies towards Africa and the Third World.

Hanna Diamond is Senior Lecturer in French History and European Studies at Bath University. She writes and teaches on the history and memory of France during the Second World War and on women in contemporary France, and is now working on the history of the mining communities in the south of France.

Claire Gorrara is Senior Lecturer in French at Cardiff University. Her research and teaching interests centre on French women's writing, French literature and culture relating to the Second World War and post-war French crime fiction.

David Hanley is Professor of European Studies at Cardiff University. His main teaching and research interests are French politics and comparative European politics, in particular parties and political systems, and European security policy.

Nigel Harkness is Lecturer in French at Queen's University, Belfast. He teaches and researches widely on nineteenth-century French literature, in particular issues of gender and writing and the work of George Sand.

Cheryl Koos is a Professor in the History Department of California State University, Los Angeles. Her research centres mainly on gender and nationalism in inter-war France. She is currently completing a book on French pro-natalist policy between 1919 and 1945.

Rachael Langford is Lecturer in French at Cardiff University. She teaches and researches on late nineteenth-century French fiction, particularly the work of Jules Vallès, and on Francophone African fiction and film.

Nick Parsons is Senior Lecturer in French at Cardiff University. His research and teaching interests focus on French and British industrial relations, comparative industrial relations, urban governance in France and contemporary French politics.

Acknowledgements

This book has been a collaborative enterprise and owes much to the kind help and support of colleagues and friends in Cardiff and elsewhere. First of all, we would like to thank colleagues in the School of European Studies at Cardiff University, particularly the French Section. Special thanks go to Gordon Cumming, Nick Parsons, and David Hanley who submitted chapters and bore with the often hectic schedule of drafting and writing. Thanks too go to Hanna Diamond whose helpful comments at the beginning of the writing process helped us find our way in a vast topic area; and to Catherine Léglu of Bristol University French Department for her expert and express translation advice. All our contributors in the UK and the USA have been very supportive and provided insightful analyses in their chapters. We would also like to thank the editors at Arnold, especially Eva Martinez, who answered queries and gave good advice at various stages.

This book makes use of extracts to support ideas and debates on the Republic in France and all sources have been referenced in the text. We would particularly like to thank *L'Express* for permission to reproduce extracts from recent articles relating to the parity debate. The copyright for such material remains with them. Where translations of texts were available, these have been used and referenced. All other translations are our own. We have tried to remain as close to the spirit and meaning of the original French text as possible. Any errors are our own.

This book would not have been possible without the help and inspiration of several important people. Claire would like to dedicate this book to Solange Pierrat-Dané and Juliette Dané. Discussions with Solange over the years have shaped the ways she has interpreted France, its culture and history. She hopes Juliette, aged ten, will one day relate to the book and the narratives it provides. Rachael would like to dedicate the book to Chris Johnes with love and many thanks for his perceptiveness and patience; to Manon Johnes with love; and to the memory of Henri and Marie-Dominique Roy.

Introduction: France and the Republic since 1789

Claire Gorrara and Rachael Langford

France is a Republic. This means that France's Head of State, the French President, is an elected representative of the French people. The fact that France is a Republic headed by a President may seem insignificant: many other nations, such as the USA for example, are also Republics. But, prior to 1789, France was not a Republic, and during the events of the French Revolution of 1789–99 French people struggled bitterly against one another to have their country become a Republic. Even more significantly, France has struggled since then to remain a Republic. In fact, Republican government only triumphed durably in France less than 150 years ago. It is the ferocity and enduring nature of the battle to root Republican values in French society and government that have made the Republic such a vital element of contemporary French identity. To date, France has been ruled by five Republics, the most recent being the Fifth Republic, created in 1958 and continuing today. It represents the current shape of democratic government in France.

This book sets out to explore the changes and developments associated with the history of the Republic in France. The chapters seek to show overall how, since 1789, each successive incarnation of the Republic has been formed in response to, and shaped by, very different historical circumstances. Each chapter focuses on a key date, a historical 'flash-point' that has had a major impact on French Republicanism. These specific locations in time and history are the 'contexts' of France since 1789 that this volume has in its subtitle. As a complement to these historical contexts, each chapter also presents the reader with 'texts', literary and documentary extracts included with a translation at the end of each chapter. These 'texts' aim to give a snapshot impression of the ways in which individuals and groups experienced and interpreted such key moments in the history of France's Republics, and to give an insight into contemporary thinking and debates. For the same reason, selected chapters also contain boxed biographies of individuals or groups of individuals touched by the events under discussion. These are included to give a flavour of the ways in which, from 1789 to the present, national historical events in the French

Republic have intersected with and impacted upon the lives of the French people.

At the end of this volume readers will find a broad time chart covering important dates in the history of France since 1789. They will also find a glossary of names giving short biographical summaries of the names highlighted in bold in each chapter. These two sections are included to help readers situate these people more easily in the period in question. But it should be borne in mind that this volume does not aim to provide a comprehensive account of the history of France since 1789. Readers can turn to more conventional textbooks for such accounts, and suggestions to help readers explore French history more thoroughly are given in the notes on further reading included at the end of each chapter. Rather, this volume aims to help both teachers and students of France to evaluate the changing fortunes of the Republic as an institution of democratic government, and as a fundamental component of French people's sense of individual and collective identity. As a prelude to this, this Introduction will briefly map the coordinates of these founding Republican values and the debates which have marked their presence in French society.

THE REPUBLIC OF 1789 AND ITS LEGACY

The birth of the Republic in France has its roots in social and political changes that were taking place in France in the eighteenth century. Towards the end of the eighteenth century, people became critical of the way in which their King, **Louis XVI**, his ministers and the French nobility were ruling France. The late eighteenth century in Europe as a whole was a period of intellectual and scientific innovation. New forms of knowledge and enquiry came to the fore, and begged difficult questions of accepted understandings of the world. In particular, non-religious world-views gained currency. Atheism struck at the heart of social and political organizations, for French monarchs ruled by 'divine right': a monarch was considered to be God's appointed representative on earth. Once the existence and nature of God were questioned, such a social and political system began to seem increasingly arbitrary. In addition, the eighteenth century saw the rapid growth of a successful middle class that was educated and wealthy, but not represented in the structures of political power. This class had the time, money and education to question its exclusion from power.

Discontent spilled out from 1789 to 1799 in events which came to be known collectively as the French Revolution. Different groups of French people fought to change, reform or maintain the way that France was governed. Many people wanted the French monarchy to continue to rule, but for it to be advised by representatives of the French people. Others felt that the monarchy was too compromised to remain involved in the government of

France. This second group did not want France to be governed by the privileged few whose land, titles and family background gave them power irrespective of their personal qualities. They wished to see people included in the government of France because of their abilities rather than their background, and they pushed hard for the abolition of the monarchy. These views eventually won. In 1793 Louis XVI was guillotined, and the monarchy and its system of government by rank and privilege were proclaimed dead. France was declared a Republic for the first time.

One of the most significant events of the French Revolution was the 'Declaration of the Rights of Man and the Citizen' of 1789, a document setting out the founding values of the hoped-for new political order. It was drawn up by those who contested the 'divine right' of kings and it set out the principles which were to become core values of French Republicanism. It declared that all men were *free citizens* of France, not subservient subjects of the monarch. All men were also *equal* before the law, so no man could be treated differently because of his social rank. Moreover, this freedom and equality led to brotherhood. Not only was every man a free citizen, equal in rights to other men, but, further, he was joined to his fellow citizens by a fraternal social bond, brotherhood, which implied reciprocal rights and duties. These core values were enshrined in the Republican slogan: *liberté, égalité, fraternité*, that is, freedom, equality, brotherhood.

The Revolution of 1789 profoundly marked French society and politics, but the Republic did not last. In the wake of the Revolution, France was a deeply divided nation. The Revolution had set up political fault lines and installed political traditions which continue to characterize Left, Right and Centre in France even today. In the first years of the nineteenth century, many French people looked back with nostalgia to the times when France had political stability and international influence, times which, they felt, had been destroyed by the Revolution of 1789. General **Napoléon Bonaparte** appeared to such people as a saviour.

Napoléon Bonaparte had become a national hero during the wars that France engaged in during the Revolution. Many saw him as a man of action and integrity who would sweep aside the political corruption which characterized Revolutionary France in the late 1790s. At the end of 1799, Napoléon became First Consul, a position of the utmost power in the government. In 1804, he was given this position for life and crowned Emperor of France.

Napoléon was an authoritarian figure with little patience for debate, and whose legacy to France has been a particular inflection of the values of 1789. For, although Napoléon's Empire had its roots in the Revolution and accepted the Revolution's principles of equality before the law and equality of opportunity, other rights and freedoms were trampled underfoot. The Napoleonic Empire (1804–14) was in essence a dictatorship that exaggerated the centralizing tendencies of the later years of the Revolution and held the ethical foundations behind the values of 1789 in contempt. Meritocracy reigned, applying a restricted form of equality. But all political power was concentrated in the Emperor's hands, freedom was curtailed (freedom of speech and assembly, for example), and brotherhood was submerged as Napoléon exploited France in pursuit of military glory.

So, by the early years of the nineteenth century, two strong but competing models for the government of post-Revolutionary France were in place. The first was based on the values of 1789 and the brotherhood of man, the second was based on the Napoléonic model of a hero-leader at the centre of all power. The struggle between these two models over the following two centuries demonstrates the extent to which Republican values in France have remained subject to contestation. For while the founding ideals of 1789 – *liberté, égalité, fraternité* – are still in use today, enshrined in the official seals of the Republic, Napoléon's inflection of these values towards a heavily centralized state and hero-leader left France with a model of governance which fundamentally contested these Republican values. For the Napoleonic model can be seen to have been resurrected under anti-Republican regimes, such as the Vichy regime during the Second World War. It also influenced important figures such as General **de Gaulle**, architect of the current Fifth Republic, in their understanding of the role of the Head of the French State. Paradoxically, therefore, it can be seen that French Revolutionary Republicanism engendered models of governance which have profoundly challenged the Republic.

But it can be argued that the vital founding document of the French Revolution and French Republicanism, the 1789 'Declaration of the Rights of Man and the Citizen', also engendered challenges to French Republicanism. For its conceptual framework contained key exclusions, 'blind spots' which, when made visible, questioned the validity of the very principles upon which French Republicanism was based. These 'blind spots' concerned the position of women; questions of cultural and religious difference; and questions of economic difference. They may be broadly distilled under the headings of gender, race and class, and they recur as challenging motifs in the history of the French Republic. It is these themes in particular that the contributors to this volume have chosen to highlight in their individual explorations of France and the Republic since 1789. The following paragraphs outline the overall historical coordinates of these key exclusions in French Republicanism, and set out some of the ways in which these themes are explored in the chapters of this book.

THEMES AND DEBATES ON THE REPUBLIC: A HISTORICAL OVERVIEW

Women, equality, citizenship

As we saw above, the founding text of the French Revolution was the 'Declaration of the Rights of Man and the Citizen' of 1789. Modelled on the

American 'Declaration of Independence' of 1776, this document declared every man a citizen (not a subject) with equal rights before the law. It thus constituted a radical rejection of the age-old hierarchies of rights which had structured pre-Revolutionary France.

Before long, however, advanced women of the day noted the exclusively masculine turn of the document. They pointed out that women could be guillotined for their opinions, but had no right to political representation, and that women were possessions, not individuals in their own right, before the law. The exclusively male terminology on which Republican values were built had important repercussions. The position of women in France from the Revolution onwards is one of the key themes of this volume, and gives an insight into how far successive French Republics have been committed to the notion of equality.

Real women and their views and demands were problematic to French Republicanism from the very beginning. From 1789 onwards, French politicians enacted laws and created institutions which betrayed a deep-seated mistrust of French women. Part of the reason for this lay in beliefs, widely held until the early twentieth century, that women were the weaker sex destined for domestic life and procreation and not suited to intellectual work or involvement in public life. But there are also reasons specific to France which explain why French Republicans were suspicious of women.

Behind many of France's civil institutions lurked the ghost of the post-Revolutionary legal code that set down France's core laws, the *Code Napoléon* of 1804. The Code was not completely reactionary, but it did legislate for the repression of women in many domains and remained in force throughout the nineteenth century. Under the Code, women had the same legal status as children; the Code stated for example that, 'a husband owes protection to his wife; a wife owes obedience to her husband'. Such legislation strongly coloured Republican thinking on women's rights, even though, having been drawn up under Napoléon Bonaparte's rule, it was the product of an anti-Republican regime.

In addition, many French Republicans feared the political conservatism of French women, who were considered to be more supportive of traditional values than men of the same social class. Many Republican politicians felt that women voting *en masse* would put an end to any Republican regime. Paradoxically, however, some Republicans also feared what they saw as the political extremism of working-class women, demonstrated during the French Revolution in 1848 (see Chapter 2), and again during the Paris Commune (see Chapter 3). During these periods of social upheaval, women came on to the streets and were involved in at times violent political protests in pursuit of more radical forms of Republicanism.

By the end of the nineteenth century, a more moderate form of Republicanism dominated the political scene in France. This moderate Republic represented itself in allegorical form as 'Marianne', a powerful but quiescent classical female figure still used to symbolize the French state today, for example, on postage stamps. Historians have noted, however, that although the cardinal Republican ideals were symbolized in female form the history of real women in the French Republic has predominantly been one of exclusion.

The momentum for women's rights, and in particular the right to vote, increased significantly at the beginning of the twentieth century, partly driven by the campaigning of women themselves. However, the battle for greater equality between the sexes was won largely due to the impact of wider social and economic forces. With the pace of industrialization, women came to dominate important sectors of the workforce and pressure was exerted to improve women's social, legal and working rights. Women's contribution to the war economy during the First World War demonstrated the pivotal role they could play in times of crisis (see Chapter 5).

This did not immediately translate into political rights. During the inter-war years, representatives in the National Assembly voted repeatedly for women's suffrage, only to be defeated by conservative forces in the indirectly elected second chamber of the French parliament, the Senate. Thus, it was not until the Liberation of France in 1944 that women gained the right to vote (see Chapter 6). This came many years after universal and female suffrage in other developed democracies, such as New Zealand (1893), Germany (1918), the United Kingdom (1918), Belgium (1919) and America (1920).

Since the first votes for women in France, the post-war period has seen many advances in terms of women's personal rights, such as the *loi Neuwirth* which legalized abortion, as well as legislation to combat sexual discrimination at work and in public life. Most recently, the campaign for *parité* (political parity) has resulted in the acceptance of a principle of equal representation for men and women in public office (see Chapter 9). In June 1999, the French Constitution was amended to contain a form of words supporting equal access for men and women in the exercise of political power. The heated discussions about *parité* encouraged a reassessment of the notion of equality within the French Republic. Should the Republic cater for the needs of all its citizens, with no reference to their individual circumstances? Or should the Republic treat women as citizens apart, due to the centuries of discrimination they had suffered? As France moves into the twenty-first century, French Republicanism continues to assess and reassess the thorny issue of women's place within public life.

Race, religion, immigration

If the Declaration of 1789 overtly excluded women, there was nothing in it overtly excluding non-European men in French territories from enjoying the rights it declared as belonging to every man. But promoting racial equality was not a central preoccupation of the Revolution. France at this time was a major colonial nation, and its overseas possessions were its treasure chest. On Caribbean islands such as Haiti, hundreds of thousands of Africans were enslaved under French rule on plantations of sugar, coffee, cocoa and cotton owned by a minority of white colonists and people of mixed racial descent. In the summer of 1791 the Haitian slaves rebelled and demanded that the 'Declaration of the Rights of Man and the Citizen' be applied to them too. Fearing it would lose its colonial possessions, France abolished slavery in all its territories in 1794.

But this abolition was short-lived. Under Napoléon Bonaparte, slavery was reinstated in all French possessions apart from Haiti (which won its independence in 1804 by successfully defeating French forces sent to crush Haitian independence). Slavery was finally abolished in 1848 under the French Second Republic (see Chapter 2). But France remained a colonial nation until well after the end of the Second World War, and full decolonization was a painful process for the French (see Chapter 7).

Here again, French Republicanism is paradoxical. The 'Declaration of the Rights of Man and the Citizen' pronounced all men to be citizens with the right to political representation and equality before the law. However, through economic and political self-interest, the Republic was unwilling to accord these same rights to the indigenous men of its colonies. In common with other colonial nations such as Britain and Belgium, it was only slowly, in the face of increasing rebelliousness by native populations, that some rights were ceded by the French Republic to its overseas possessions (see Chapter 7). The most recent of these was the right to self-government. This last process was at times an extremely bloody one, as the events of the Algerian war for independence from France (1954–62) bear out.

French Republicanism's historical difficulties in accepting that men and women of non-Western culture qualify for the rights of French citizenship has had knock-on effects on the Republic's attitude to its immigrant populations. One of the main challenges here has stemmed from the secular nature of the French State. A founding act of modern French Republicanism was the formal separation of Church and State in 1905, a move which aimed to weaken the power of the Roman Catholic Church in France and deny it influence over state institutions, such as the school (see Chapter 4). By this act, French citizens were free to follow any religion they wished in their private lives, but there was to be no state religion and religious symbols and observances were to play no part in public life. Two of the groups most implicated in this process of integrating different faith communities into French secular public life have been Jews and Muslims.

One of the early victories of the French Revolution was to define French citizenship as an act of will and not as the result of blood ties or vague racial criteria. This led in 1791 to the emancipation of Jews living in France. From this time onwards, Jews became closely associated with the Revolution's Republican values. In exchange for acceptance and proper integration into

French life, they endorsed the French nation and its Republican traditions over Jewish religious and cultural practices. Yet, by the late nineteenth century, anti-Semitism was never far off the political and cultural agenda. With the **Dreyfus** affair of the 1890s in France (see Chapter 4), the French Republic's principles of racial and religious tolerance were severely compromised as French nationalists used anti-Semitic stereotypes to scapegoat Jews for all of France's social and political ills. Such anti-Semitism reached its zenith during the Second World War, with the Vichy regime's complicity in the arrest and deportation of Jews to extermination camps in Eastern Europe (see Chapter 6).

The secular nature of the French State has also led to conflicts between the French authorities and the Muslim population of France, particularly in the post-war period. For Muslim communities, the public sphere is in no way exempt from the duties of religious observance. The clash between this view of public life and French secularism is evident from conflicts such as the *affaire du foulard* (the headscarf controversy) of 1989. Muslim girls demanded the right to wear their traditional headscarves to state schools, but were excluded from school by the French authorities because the *foulard* was taken to be a religious symbol. In the end, the French authorities inventively made their way out of the difficulty by accepting the *foulard* as a cultural, rather than a religious, item.

Thus the ideals of the French Republic have often stood in contradiction to the reality of France's colonial and post-colonial interventions on the international stage (see Chapter 7), and to its treatment of cultural difference within its borders. Abroad, France's wish to play a prominent part in international politics has impacted on national sovereignties by discouraging francophone identities which do not look to the French Republic as their natural ally. In France itself, Republicanism's inability to integrate multiculturalism and cultural differences has led to overtly racist views entering mainstream politics. The extremist anti-immigration politics of the *Front National* (National Front) continue to enjoy a bedrock of support in the Republic even in 2002.

Thus, while it is true to say that immigration and multiculturalism will pose difficulties for all nations in contemporary Europe in the next decades, they nevertheless pose particular problems for the French Republic. It remains to be seen whether, in the face of continuing economic and political change, the Republic will find strategies which can meet the challenge of guaranteeing basic freedoms to those with different religious and ethnic traditions residing in France.

Class, conflict, work

One of the main legacies of the French Revolution was that political rights and representation were no longer to be linked to money, property or influence. All men (and women subsequently), irrespective of their class origins, had the right to express their views in public life. For Republicans who believed that social and economic reform were as important as the reform of political institutions, this led them to question the unequal distribution of wealth in France and the privileges that money bestowed. Such views informed the revolutions of 1848 and 1871 (see Chapters 2 and 3). These revolutions saw more radical Republicans seeking social reforms which would improve the lives of the impoverished classes in France. Informed by international events, such as the Russian Revolution of 1917, and by the social and economic changes of the twentieth century, currents of left-leaning Republicanism continued to have lively support in France throughout the twentieth century.

However, the concern with improving the lives of the vast majority of workers pitted bourgeois and middle-class interests against those of the urban and rural poor. The latter's demands for improvements in social and economic conditions threatened the commercial interests of the former; and urban workers in particular felt exploited and excluded from power. These feelings of exclusion contributed to the outbreak of the Paris Commune of 1871 (see Chapter 3) and to the events of May 1968, when student protests burst out to mobilize over 11 million workers to strike (see Chapter 8).

Yet, despite deep-seated fears over the rebellious potential of urban workers, succeeding Republics came to rely heavily on the French workforce: the Republic needed productive and contented workers, both men and women, for economic growth and stability. One of the Republic's greatest successes was in binding workers to an inclusive concept of the Republic in the aftermath of the Paris Commune of 1871. The Commune shook middle-class confidence in the working class to its foundations (see Chapter 3). But the numbers of young working-class men who volunteered for combat during the First World War testifies to the success of subsequent government efforts in eliding class interests in favour of national ones, and fostering the notion that defence of the Republic equalled defence of the nation (see Chapter 5). The connections between industrialization, worker participation and the French Republic were brought home even more forcefully during the short-lived Vichy regime during the Second World War. The urban worker as a class hero, agent of left-wing change, and most importantly as a resistance activist, was anathema to the programme of national renewal set up by the anti-Republican Vichy regime (see Chapter 6).

As socio-economic conditions have changed over time, so have the ways in which class has been understood in France. The previously polarized categories of the 'bourgeois' and the 'worker' have shifted to designate different groupings with changing concerns and aspirations. The success of the *Parti Communiste Français* (French Communist Party, PCF) was based on politically literate communities of voters in the industrial heartlands of northern and eastern France who identified themselves as working class. The PCF was at the height of its powers in the late 1940s, forming coalitions with Centre–Left parties during the Fourth Republic. But the rapid decline of traditional manufacturing industries in the post-1945 era and the fall of Communism in

Eastern Europe have both contributed to the erosion of such sure class allegiances. New forms of negotiation and worker–employer relations have had to be conceived, some of which have been underpinned by state intervention, such as the recent introduction of the 35-hour working week (see Chapter 8).

The concept of a united, militant working class is on the wane. Commentators in France now focus on new activist movements, framed in part by new forms of social exclusion, where poverty, rather than work, is the defining factor. The decline in traditional forms of worker-participation in French public life may be because French workers consider the current Fifth Republic to have fulfilled the Revolutionary promise of economic, social and political equality. But it may also be that political protesters have abandoned the traditional Revolutionary model, even as recently as May 1968. For French class allegiances have shifted, and have done so in response to international economic developments as much as to domestic ones. It may be now that the aspiration to belong to the middle-classes has triumphed over collective hopes to champion social change.

CONCLUSION

This introduction has explored some of the ways in which debates on gender, race and class have challenged French Republican values. These intersecting identities do not constitute an exhaustive list of the identities which pose problems for French Republicanism, and it would be difficult to understand the triumph of French Republicanism without reference to the wider world. What of France's long history of animosity and conflict with Germany, for long the traditional enemy? And what of the United States, whose 'Declaration of Independence' in 1776 was the model for France's 'Declaration of the Rights of Man and the Citizen'? Today, the USA is a global economic competitor who inspires admiration but also mistrust. France's choices in the alliances it makes as part of the new European and world order in the wake of 11 September 2001 will also indelibly mark the future of French Republicanism.

As you read this book, we hope that you will be stimulated to discover and discuss how Republican values have shaped contemporary French identity. Since the definitive endorsement of the French Republic in the years 1875–80, not a year has gone by without the Republic being questioned, threatened, modified, pulled to the Left or to the Right. As the accompanying document shows, the French Republic has always had to face the accusation that it extends its cardinal values of freedom, equality and brotherhood to some and not to all. It has been seen to privilege certain groups at the expense of others; to promise more than it can deliver; to betray the true nature of the French nation and its centuries-long history. And yet the French Republic remains remarkably enduring.

Extract 1: Maurice Agulhon, a notable historian of French
Republicanism, on a discussion in the late nineteenth century

Un conseiller avait proposé que le nom de Place de la République, et la
statue correspondante, soient attribués à la Place de la Concorde. Celle-
ci étant devenue le centre géographique et esthétique de Paris, le fait d'y
planter la République aurait clairement manifesté qu'elle régnait sur la
capitale et sur le pays. Mais . . . d'autres conseillers tout aussi radicaux
trouvèrent au contraire très heureux que la République soit mise dans les
quartiers de l'Est, au voisinage de ses meilleurs amis. Mais n'était-ce pas
se résigner à en faire la déesse d'une moitié de capitale, et d'une moitié de
France?

Source: Maurice Agulhon, 1979: Marianne au combat, l'imagerie et la
symbolique républicaines de 1789 à 1880. Paris: Flammarion, p. 222

One councillor had suggested that the name of the *Place de la
République,* and the corresponding statue, should be given to the *Place
de la Concorde.* This latter having become the geographical and aesthetic
centre of Paris, planting the Republic there would clearly have
demonstrated that she reigned over the capital and the country. But . . .
other, equally radical, councillors thought on the contrary that it was
very suitable that the Republic should be put in the eastern districts, in
the neighbourhood of her best friends. But wasn't this to resign oneself to
making the Republic the goddess of only half the capital, and half of
France?

FURTHER READING

Agulhon, M. 1979. *Marianne au combat, l'imagerie et la symbolique
   républicaines de 1789 à 1880.* Paris: Flammarion.
   A lively account of Republicanism and its symbols from the Revolution
   until the early Third Republic.
Alexander, M. (ed.) 1999. *French history since Napoléon.* London: Arnold.
   Scholarly and informative essays on themes and debates in nineteenth- and
   twentieth-century French history.
Gildea, R. 1996. *France since 1945.* Oxford: Oxford University Press.
   Concise and original introduction to French history since 1945, taking a
   thematic rather than chronological approach to its material.
Kidd, W. and Reynolds, S. (eds) 2000. *Contemporary French cultural studies.*
   London: Arnold.

A historical and context-based introduction to contemporary French cultural identity, structured around key areas such as politics, language, cinema and education.

Morris, P. 1994. *French politics today*. Manchester: Manchester University Press.

Clear and readable analysis of institutions, events and trends which have shaped the modern French political scene.

Nora, P. (ed.) 1992. *Lieux de mémoire* (3 vols). Paris: Gallimard. Translated by Arthur Goldhammer and edited by Lawrence Kritzman as *Realms of memory*. New York: Columbia University Press.

Highly influential collection examining shared national values in French history and culture, containing a wealth of insights.

1

The French Revolution: origins and beginnings

Hanna Diamond

INTRODUCTION

The French Revolution was a founding moment in French history. Its repercussions were felt throughout Europe. It brought the end of the old feudal system of government in France. Archaic laws were swept away and the government of the country was recreated by the laws and decrees introduced during the Revolutionary period. The First Republic declared in 1792 was short-lived, but its influence and the principles it enshrined were long-lasting. Republicanism was to have a profound impact on French politics and society from that time forward. This chapter will explore both the key events of the French Revolution and the foundations of French Republicanism, and it will focus on one of the key tensions in the Republican ideal, the issue of women in society.

BACKGROUND TO THE REVOLUTION

In eighteenth-century Europe in general, society was organized in a static and hierarchical way. The French monarchy of this time was an absolute monarchy, which presided over a feudal system based on centuries of accumulated precedent in relations between the monarch, the aristocracy and the clergy. The unquestionable right of the French monarch to rule was part of this tradition: the monarch was believed to have a 'divine right' to govern because his royal status was an incarnation of God's will.

This system of government was known as the *ancien régime* in France. Under it, the King and his councillors had all the power. There were no elected representatives, and the organization of society was blatantly unjust: tax burdens fell particularly heavily on the poor, as feudal laws exempted churchmen and the aristocracy from having to pay most taxes.

French society under the *ancien régime* was organized hierarchically in a class system known as the Three Estates. The First Estate was that of the clergy who were relatively prosperous as the Church was extremely wealthy: it was the single largest landowner in France, owning about 10 per cent of the land. The Church amassed its wealth by collecting tithes from people living on its land (tithes were a proportion of each year's crops, about 8 per cent, which had to be given freely to the landowner). The Second Estate, comprised of the nobility or the aristocracy, was also well off. This group was the most powerful in French society and they owned about a third of all the land in France. The Third Estate, however, represented everyone else, about 90 per cent of the population. This included the bourgeoisie, the peasants, and the urban merchants and workers. The Third Estate was the least favoured group in eighteenth-century France in terms of material comfort and security.

Between 1740 and 1783, France had been at war for 20 years, with Austria, and in the American War of Independence. These campaigns were costly and led the government to borrow on a large scale. The situation was aggravated by internal economic crisis. Poor harvests had led to higher bread prices and high unemployment levels, which caused considerable discontent. It was the financial bankruptcy of the French monarchy under **Louis XVI** that triggered the events of the Revolution. In 1789, the King went to his aristocracy and explained to them that he was introducing tax reform in order to attempt to deal with the national debt. But the nobles were aware of their political power in such a situation and they resisted Louis' demand that they too should provide revenue for France by paying tax. Instead they forced him to call the Estates General into session.

This body consisted of elected representatives from all of France's Three Estates. It had not sat since 1614. The calling for a session of the Estates General unleashed forces which neither the King nor the nobles could control, for the disgruntled Third Estate did not intend to let the monarchy and the aristocracy decide the future of the nation.

The King had asked each Estate to bring to the meeting of the Estates General lists of their grievances and hopes for change. It turned out that the grievances of all three orders had many themes in common. All were against absolute royal power and all wanted a king whose powers would be limited by an elected assembly with the right to vote on taxes and on laws. So the King and his ministers found themselves faced with a dilemma. They could not satisfy demands for a larger share of the political power and a smaller burden of tax without destroying the feudal rights of the nobles and the Church, which largely exempted these two groups from taxation. And they could not do this without sacrificing some of their own power and changing the whole structure of France, altering the essential character of the old order in which their authority was embedded. But the Estates, and the Third Estate in particular, felt that the time had come for change. The expectation on all sides was that Louis would get the financial relief he wanted in return for addressing the grievances of the Estates General.

THE EVENTS OF THE REVOLUTION

1789–1791: The Declaration of the Rights of Man and the writing of a new Constitution

Not long after its first meeting on 17 June, divisions over voting rights between the Three Estates led the Third Estate alone to declare itself a National Assembly. On 20 June, with the passing of the *Serment du Jeu de Paume* (the Tennis Court Oath), this Assembly pledged not to disband until it had given France a Constitution, thus claiming that the King did not have the right to dissolve it. On 27 June, in order to calm growing popular unrest, the King ordered the nobility and clergy to work with this new National Assembly, which, on 9 July, termed itself the National Constituent Assembly to underline its role. The National Constituent Assembly was hoping to negotiate a constitutional monarchy, where representative government would share power with the monarchy. But the King refused to cooperate with any of the Assembly's propositions and he appeared to be amassing troops to dissolve it forcibly.

At this point, events began to take on a momentum of their own. On 14 July 1789, a crowd of over 800 people marched to the Bastille, an ancient Paris prison felt to symbolize the oppression of the people. The crowd stormed it and formed their own citizens' militia, known as the Paris National Guard, to protect the city from any attack by royal troops. Largely in reaction to reports of these events in the capital, demonstrations and riots against feudal taxes spread throughout the country. It appeared increasingly that law and order had collapsed across France. All these events compounded the sense that the country was out of control.

In the Assembly session of 4 August 1789, in an attempt to calm this disorder, a number of nobles and churchmen gave up their feudal rights and a decree was announced supporting equality between citizens. The National Constituent Assembly decided that, before writing its new constitution for France, it should set forth a statement of broad principles. On 26 August, representatives produced the *Déclaration des Droits de l'Homme et du Citoyen* (Declaration of the Rights of Man and the Citizen), an extract of which is included at the end of this chapter. This Declaration became the founding document not only for the Revolution, but also for the French Republican movement as a whole. It roundly condemned the practices of the old order and reflected the demands for change advocated by the Three Estates.

The Declaration was drawn up by **La Fayette**. It contained ideas about essential human freedoms from the American Declaration of Independence (1776), as well as from the Bill of Rights (1689) passed in Britain in the aftermath of the 'Glorious Revolution' of 1688. It consisted of a preamble setting out its reasons for existence, and 17 articles listing every individual's natural and inalienable rights. These rights formed the basis for a new relationship between the individual and society. The Declaration affirmed the universal nature of human rights. Sovereignty shifted from the King, an absolute monarch, to the nation, which could not be divided into orders. No individual could claim absolute power. These rights were to be written into law, an expression of the general will, and decided by the citizen's vote. The men who collaborated on the Declaration were not thinking just of France, but of men everywhere who wanted to be free and rid themselves of the burdens of absolutist monarchy and feudal privilege. The Declaration of the Rights of Man and the Citizen remained the charter of political liberalism throughout the nineteenth century.

The King delayed ratifying the new Constitution based on the Declaration, and there was concern that he might use his troops to defend his position. On 5 October 1789, 7,000 hungry Parisian women marched on the Assembly and to the royal palace at Versailles, demanding food. Many of the women stayed in the palace overnight. The King was obliged to relocate to the Tuileries Palace in central Paris where he could be more closely watched, and from 6 October Paris became the main stage for the key events of the Revolution.

Throughout 1790 and 1791 the Revolution radicalized. In response to increasing financial bankruptcy, and in line with revolutionary anti-clericalism, Church lands were nationalized and sold off, monasteries and convents were dissolved, and in July 1790 the Civil Constitution of the Clergy required churchmen to swear allegiance to the new political order. Alarmed by this growing radicalism, on 20 September 1791 the King and his family attempted to flee France and enlist support from foreign powers, particularly Austria. But the royal family were caught and brought back to Paris. Under pressure, Louis agreed to sign the new Constitution on 14 September 1791.

The Constitution of 1791 provided for a constitutional monarchy, with real power vested in an elected assembly. The King retained the right to appoint his ministers and military commanders, but his power was subordinate to the elected assembly, which could pass laws the King was obliged to obey.

The anti-clerical laws of 1790 had already unleashed powerful counter-revolutionary forces in defence of the Church and, by extension, of the monarchy. But the royal family's attempt to escape France and call on other powers to go to war with the country to support the French monarchy lost them much popular support. As politics polarized, the mood among revolutionaries changed from one of tolerance for a monarchy with limited powers to a desire to be rid of the King once and for all. The Legislative Assembly, voted in on 1 October 1791 following the signing of the Constitution, was far less sympathetic to the King than the preceding National Assembly and National Constituent Assembly had been.

1792–95: From radical Republic to reactionary Republic

On 20 April 1792, Revolutionary France declared war on Austria and Prussia. This step was seen as necessary to defend the Revolution. It is likely that the

King hoped France would lose this war so that he could then re-establish himself in power. And indeed the war began to go very badly for Revolutionary France: by August 1792, Prussian and Austrian forces had crossed the French border and were heading towards Paris.

Within the Revolutionary government itself, the situation became ever more complicated. There was much jockeying for political ascendancy between the different factions involved in government, and war had to be fought on two fronts: internally against supporters of the monarchy and the clergy, and externally against the hostile foreign powers. At about this time, the radical revolutionaries known as Jacobins gained the upper hand in Revolutionary government, until then dominated by a more moderate group, the Girondists (most of them were from the *Gironde* department). The Jacobins had been active in political discussion clubs from the very beginning of the Revolution, and their support was particularly strong in Paris. They decried social privilege, were anti-clerical and favoured a liberal economic policy. To them, the very existence of a French King was a threat to the success of the Revolution in France. They felt that a constitutional monarchy was a weak compromise, and they called for its complete abolition. On 10 August 1792, the Tuileries palace was stormed by the Paris National Guard. The King's personal guard was massacred and the royal family was arrested and imprisoned. The Legislative Assembly, faced with a series of crushing military defeats and constantly pressurized by the radical Paris activists, made way for the government called the *Convention Nationale*.

The first act of the Convention was to declare France a Republic, on 22 September 1792, and it continued in a similar vein: in December 1792, Louis was tried for 'conspiracy against public liberty' and was found guilty by 387 votes to 334. He was sentenced to death, and executed in January 1793 as Louis Capet, a common traitor. But the demands of the Revolutionary wars, internal and external, led to the Convention's real power being hived off into a kind of war cabinet, a 12-man Committee of Public Safety controlled by the Jacobins.

This Committee was dominated first by **Danton** and then by **Robespierre**, two formidable orators and supporters of radical revolutionary measures, the latter more extreme than the former. Now a period of remarkably successful campaigns to protect the Revolution from other European nations (including Britain) was begun, and within France itself the Committee of Public Safety sanctioned extreme penalties for any counter-revolutionary activity. The period known as the Terror raged, as 'enemies' of the Revolution were executed increasingly summarily: in this period, over 40,000 French men, women and children were put to death for suspected counter-revolutionary sympathies.

But the balance of power in the Revolutionary government shifted again. Danton and his associates were denounced and executed in April 1793 for questioning the purposes of the Terror. And, in late July 1794, Robespierre was arrested and executed by his opponents just as he seemed to be on the point of absolute dictatorship. Reaction to radical Republicanism had begun, and throughout 1795 there was much anti-Jacobin repression, as well as isolated radical Republican uprisings. In some areas, supporters of the monarchy also caused much unrest.

1795–1804: Ending the Revolution

The Convention drafted a new constitution in an attempt to preserve the ideals of 1789 against both reactionary monarchists and radical Republicans. The *Constitution de l'An III de la Révolution* (the Constitution of Year III of the Revolution) set up a democratic model of government with safeguards against individual dictatorship, such as that which Robespierre had nearly achieved. There would be two elected chambers to government, and a Directorate of five men sharing a 'prime ministerial' role, who would appoint ministers and command the armed forces. But the new Constitution restricted the bases on which men were allowed to vote: voting became a privilege for the relatively wealthy once more. Overall, this period of the Revolution called the Directorate (1795–99) was marked by decadence and political corruption among the governing classes, and continuing poverty and political disenfranchisement for the rural and urban poor.

All the while, the Revolutionary wars continued abroad, and news of the successes of a brilliant young general, **Louis Napoléon Bonaparte**, were increasingly reported. In 1799, quarrels among the Directors and fear of a monarchist counter-revolution encouraged them to call on Napoléon Bonaparte, by now the most successful of the Revolution's generals, to bolster the political regime. Napoléon saw his chance to move to the centre of political power. With his *coup d'état* of November 1799, a three-man Consulate was introduced, with himself as the supremely powerful First Consul. Any shadow of representative government ended with this barely disguised dictatorship.

In May 1802, Bonaparte appointed himself First Consul for life and, in May 1804, he had himself crowned Emperor of France. Under the Napoléonic Empire, basic Republican ideals such as the freedom of speech were cast aside in favour of a form of military government which was firmly centralized in the hands of one man. The Napoléonic Empire lasted until 1814 when Napoléon abdicated. A year later, profiting from the weakness of the restored monarch **Louis XVIII**, Napoléon escaped from the island of Elba where he had been held prisoner. For a short time it looked as if he might return to lead France, but 100 days after his escape Napoléon and his armies were defeated at Waterloo by Nelson, and he abdicated for a final time.

'LA RÉPUBLIQUE SANS LES FEMMES' – EQUALITY, GENDER AND THE REVOLUTION

Before 1789, a few wealthy educated women ran literary and political salons through which they exerted an informal, but considerable, influence. A few contemporary documents claiming that women's condition could only improve if they had access to a decent education existed, and a number of works of literature interested themselves in the role and education of women. Some women writers bitterly deplored the absence of political rights for women, but to demand them outright seemed too audacious. Yet, in the documentation explaining the grievances of the people submitted to Louis XVI in 1789, there was little reference to the situation of women. Moreover, the Declaration of the Rights of Man and the Citizen more or less ignored or omitted women, and the Civil Code of 1804 that arose from it was directly repressive. Women emerged from the Revolution into the early nineteenth century not with improved political and legal rights, but with fewer.

Women played an extremely active part in the events of the Revolution and participated in the storming of the Bastille. They acted as a leading element in the food riots and demonstrations and often served to incite men to action. **Pauline Léon** also endeavoured to gain recognition for women. On 6 March 1792, she and 20 other women took a petition signed by 319 women to the National Assembly demanding that women should be allowed to organize a female National Guard carrying arms and thereby putting into practice Robespierre's affirmation on 27 April 1791 that 'to be armed for the defence of the nation is the right of all citizens'. Her efforts were in vain. Women attended men's clubs and some women's clubs were established, notably the 'Women's Club of Revolutionary Republican Citizens' founded in 1793 by Pauline Léon. In the Assembly, women occupied the public benches, and these women, who became known as *les tricoteuses* in 1795, tried to put across their ideas and influence the deputies by intervening in debates.

However, an educated minority of women realized that the Revolution was going against their interests and set out deliberately to try to rectify this. Many demanded that rights for all men should also be accorded to women. The vocabulary used in the Declaration of Rights of Man and the Citizen overlooked the status of women and reflected the ambiguous nature of women's citizenship. Women were citizens as inhabitants of France, but their citizenship did not allow them political rights in the same way as men. **Olympe de Gouges** reacted to this denial of women's rights by publishing, in September 1791, the Declaration of the Rights of Woman and the Citizeness in which she replaced 'he' with 'she' throughout the text of the Declaration of the Rights of Man and the Citizen.

Despite the attempts of women like de Gouges and Léon, the Revolution extended the exclusion of women from politics into law. There was no doubt that the revolutionaries as a whole were hostile to women. Most adopted the contemporary belief that women's natures were essentially emotional, bereft of the 'male' faculty of reasoning. Women were told that, instead of careers in public life, they should focus on raising good male citizens. These ideas were also enshrined in the Civil Code of 1804 and the equal division of property only passed on to male heirs. Married women were judged incapable of

Olympe de Gouges and the Declaration of the Rights of Woman

Olympe de Gouges (1755–93) was the daughter of a butcher and a washerwoman, and she married a wealthy older man. After becoming a widow, she had sufficient funds to support herself in Paris. Ridiculed because of her staunch unyielding feminism, she was derided as a traitor to the Revolution because of her opposition to the death of the King and his family. Although she supported the initial aims of the Revolution, she spoke out against the bloodshed of the Terror. She was guillotined in 1793 as a reactionary royalist.

The first article of her 'Declaration of the Rights of Woman and the Citizeness' proclaimed that 'Women are born free and equal to men.' She claimed equality for women with men in all aspects of both public and private life: the equal right to vote, to hold office, to public employment, to speak in public on political topics, to equal public 'honours', to own and control property, to participate in the military, to an education, and to equal power in the family and the Church. A moderate monarchist, she dedicated the text to **Marie-Antoinette**, demonstrating thus that women's condition crossed social and political differences. The difficulties arose, according to de Gouges, from the exclusion of women from politics. But it was the content of this document rather than its impact, which was relatively small, that makes it an essential feminist text.

making contracts and remained minors under the tutelage of husbands and fathers. Women's rights were actually reduced compared to pre-Revolutionary days, depriving them of control over their dowries. Thus the Revolution drove married women into the private sphere and left the public sphere very much a male domain. But, if feminism did not emerge as a real force during the Revolution, it encouraged later generations of women to search for ways of articulating their concerns for equality.

THE REVOLUTION'S LEGACY TO REPUBLICANISM

If the French Revolution offered no agreed model for subsequent regimes, the ideology that it fostered, Republicanism, remained a political force throughout the nineteenth century, to become firmly established in France's political mainstream with the retreat of monarchist threats to the Third Republic in the mid-1870s. As we have seen, key aspects of Republicanism were disputed among the revolutionaries. Nevertheless, a core of ideas and values arose out of the events of the Revolution to provide the basis of Republicanism throughout the following century.

Anti-monarchism

The monarchy was the most famous of the abandoned institutions of the *ancien régime*, and indeed Republicanism is most usually taken to mean the absence of support for hereditary, unelected rulers. The abolition of the monarchy decreed in 1792 was not immediately durable, however, for after Napoléon's demise in 1814 a different branch of the monarchy was restored to rule in France. However, it was still not the same kind of absolute monarchy as had been in place before the Revolution: the Bourbon Restoration monarchs (**Louis XVIII** who ruled from 1814 to 1824, and **Charles X**, ruling from 1824 to 1830) had their powers limited by an elected assembly which had the right to pass laws. And, indeed, the monarchs and monarchs-in-waiting of the nineteenth century might have been successful in setting France up as a permanent constitutional monarchy, had the memory of the Revolution and the continued strength of French Republicanism not had the effect of making them even more reactionary than they might have been. Thus the end of Charles X's reign in 1830 was caused by his disdain for representative government. And the pretender to the throne of the 1870s lost support because of his intransigent refusal of the Tricolour flag, brought in during the Revolution but firmly accepted as the French national flag by the 1870s. Throughout the nineteenth century, Republicanism remained a lively political force in opposition to the monarchist and Bonapartist positions. Moreover, the concept of political Left and Right was born with the Revolution. At the first meeting of the Estates General, the nobles instinctively positioned themselves to the right of the King, sitting on the right hand of authority, as on 'the right hand of God', as an established mark of privilege. Accordingly, the Third Estate was to be found to the left of the King. As a result 'the Right' became a natural term for the political establishment while 'the Left' applied to its opponents. This opposition of 'Left' and 'Right' has provided a basic metaphor for the European political spectrum ever since.

Anti-clericalism

The most contentious aspect of the Revolution was religion. Priests became salaried state officials and the State took over all Catholic Church property, most of which was sold to wealthy bourgeois revolutionaries. A Civil Constitution of the Clergy was imposed in 1790. This required the election of a reduced number of priests and bishops in a reorganization of the Catholic Church along the lines of local government. Many clerics refused to accept it. Church ceremonies for births, marriages and deaths were outlawed for a number of years, and the Committee of Public Safety even instituted a new religion of the Supreme Being. After the fall of Robespierre, Catholicism gradually regained ground. With the Concordat of 1801 between Napoleonic France and the Pope, freedom of worship for Catholics was agreed in return for certain state controls over the Church in France. The Concordat recognized Catholicism as the religion of most of the French people. Importantly though, the Church's monopoly was permanently broken in the field of education. For, under Napoléon's Empire, education was reorganized into the current system of centralized state schooling, based on a ministry in Paris and *lycées* (secondary schools) in major towns. This system still endures today.

The Revolution's separation of the fields of influence of Church and State in the 1790s brought to the fore the notion of a secular state, and the need for a secular state became a key tenet of Republicanism. This meant that most Republicans were not supporters of the Church, and that most members of the Catholic Church in France were not Republicans. Throughout the nineteenth century, Catholics saw Republicans as hostile persecutors; and Republicans saw the Church as a fierce enemy of the Republic, a reactionary force determined to oppose change. Despite the moves of the 1790s, full separation between the Catholic Church in France and the French State was only finally passed in 1905, testifying to the passions aroused by the issue on both Left and Right throughout the preceding century.

Nationalism

Nationalism was another powerful notion given impetus by the Revolution. At first, talk of patriotism and the nation was not aggressive towards neighbouring states: when the government went to war in 1792, it was to liberate oppressed people and defend the Revolution. Revolutionary leaders set out to produce a unified nation, hoping to break with regionalism and local variation (in laws and taxes, for example), which they saw as characteristic of the *ancien régime*. Symbols like the Tricolour (the new national flag), the *Marseillaise* (adopted as the national anthem in 1795) and huge national festivals were all used to arouse a sense of identification with the French nation.

Further, the Revolution's military campaigns led to the introduction of conscription, obliging all young men to follow a period of military service, and this too bred loyalty to France as nation. For many young men from the regions of France, their period of military service was the first time they had been outside their own locality or come into contact with the French language, for often their language and culture were predominantly regional (Breton, Occitan or Basque, for example). But the success of French Revolutionary leaders in forging dominant national loyalties should not be exaggerated. France's success in the Revolutionary wars has frequently been attributed to the Revolution's ability to mobilize people in defence of a unitary French nation, and French Republicanism long emphasized national unity over regional diversity as a key political tenet. But French regional identities and languages have been remarkably enduring.

Representative government and centralization

The representative national and local assemblies that were established during the Revolution were not really democratic in the way we understand this term today. Voting was confined to a minority of property holders. In the 1790s, the electoral system was heavily weighted in favour of the wealthy, although 61 per cent of Frenchmen had the right to take part in some elections. However, an elected legislature was to be one of the permanent changes of the Revolution. This principle was accompanied by the creation of the judicial, fiscal and educational institutions of the modern centralized French State. The administrative structure of modern France emerged: there were new regular courts of law for both criminal and civil cases, a centralized treasury, taxes from which no-one was exempt, the standardization of weights and measures. Standardized codes of laws were worked out, and exported beyond France by the conquering Revolutionary and Napoléonic armies. Hereditary nobility was abolished and under the Republic all people were citizens equal in status before the law. With the rise of Napoléon to power, the early egalitarian impulses inherent in the Revolution were abandoned in favour of advancement by merit and talent; and this Napoléonic ideal of a meritocracy, with new ranks and titles and the *Légion d'Honneur* (1802) (Legion of Honour), became incorporated into mainstream Republicanism.

In regional government, the old provinces were erased together with their historical privileges and assemblies, to be replaced by the 82 smaller districts or *départements* named after rivers or mountain ranges. These were all of comparable size with identical administrative structures. Each department was divided into districts which were in turn subdivided into communes, each with their own mayor. Taxation also changed. The old hated taxes and exemptions disappeared, but in the long run the burden of tax on the peasantry still remained considerable. It was only by systematic review and codification that the volume of legislative changes made in the 1790s could be rationalized. A new Civil Code was produced in 1804 to meet this need. The Code replaced all the 360 local codes in place in 1789, and confirmed the rights of citizenship and of equality before the law as pronounced in the Declaration of the Rights of Man and the Citizen.

CONCLUSION

The greatest influence of the Revolution was probably in terms of ideas. The idea of revolution itself was born. Before 1789, most Europeans believed in the status quo and accepted the importance of tradition. After 1789, it became apparent that men had the power to come together to effect dramatic social and political change. The concept of essential human rights was not invented by the French Revolution, but gained enormous impetus from it.

The legacy of the Revolution is still disputed. The fault lines in French society and politics that were embodied in the events of the Revolution re-emerged throughout the nineteenth century to manifest themselves in the political crises of 1830, 1848, 1870 and 1894. Indeed, some would argue that the Revolution has not even ended today because disputes over the primacy of social versus legal equality continue within French Republicanism. But the French Revolution remains a foundational moment in the French consciousness and for French Republicanism. This was eloquently demonstrated in 1989 with the bicentennial celebrations of the Revolution: President **François Mitterrand** spared no expense to organize magnificent parades on the Champs Élysées and to renovate the buildings that had been the stage for the tumultuous events of 1789.

Extract 1.1: Déclaration des Droits de l'Homme et du Citoyen, 26 août 1789

Article premier – Les hommes naissent et demeurent libres et égaux en droits. Les distinctions sociales ne peuvent être fondées que sur l'utilité commune.

Article 2 – Le but de toute association politique est la conservation des droits naturels et imprescriptibles de l'homme. Ces droits sont la liberté, la propriété, la sûreté et la résistance à l'oppression.

Article 3 – Le principe de toute souveraineté réside essentiellement dans la Nation. Nul corps, nul individu ne peut exercer d'autorité qui n'en émane expressément.

Article 4 – La liberté consiste à pouvoir faire tout ce qui ne nuit pas à autrui : ainsi, l'exercice des droits naturels de chaque homme n'a de bornes que celles qui assurent aux autres membres de la société la jouissance de ces mêmes droits. Ces bornes ne peuvent être déterminées que par la loi.

...

Article 7 – Nul homme ne peut être accusé, arrêté ou détenu que dans les cas déterminés par la loi et selon les formes qu'elle a prescrites. Ceux qui sollicitent, expédient, exécutent ou font exécuter des ordres arbitraires doivent être punis ; mais tout citoyen appelé ou saisi en vertu de la loi doit obéir à l'instant ; il se rend coupable par la résistance.

...

Article 10 – Nul ne doit être inquiété pour ses opinions, même religieuses, pourvu que leur manifestation ne trouble pas l'ordre public établi par la loi.

Article 11 – La libre communication des pensées et des opinions est un des droits les plus précieux de l'homme ; tout citoyen peut donc parler, écrire, imprimer librement, sauf à répondre de l'abus de cette liberté dans les cas déterminés par la loi.

...

Article 13 – Pour l'entretien de la force publique, et pour les dépenses d'administration, une contribution commune est indispensable ; elle doit être également répartie entre les citoyens en raison de leurs facultés.

Article 14 – Les citoyens ont le droit de constater, par eux-mêmes ou par leurs représentants, la nécessité de la contribution publique, de la consentir librement, d'en suivre l'emploi, et d'en déterminer la quotité, l'assiette, le recouvrement et la durée.

...

Article 17 – La propriété étant un droit inviolable et sacré, nul ne peut en être privé, si ce n'est lorsque la nécessité publique légalement constatée, l'exige évidemment, et sous la condition d'une juste et préalable indemnité.

Source: http://www.justice.gouv.fr/textfond/ddhc.htm

The Declaration of the Rights of Man and the Citizen, 26 August 1789

1. Men are born and remain free and equal in their rights. Social distinctions may only be founded on the common good.
2. The aim of every political association is the maintenance of the natural and imprescriptible rights of man. Those rights are those of liberty, property, security and resistance to oppression.
3. The fundamental source of all sovereignty resides in the nation. Neither any body nor any individual may wield any authority which does not stem directly from the nation.
4. Liberty consists in being able to do anything which does not harm another: thus it is that the exercise of each man's natural rights is only bounded by the limits which ensure the enjoyment of these same rights for other members of society. These limits can only be determined by the law.

...

7. No man may be accused, arrested or detained except in cases determined by the law and in the ways that the law has set out. Those

who solicit, send, carry out or have carried out for them arbitrary orders must be punished; but any citizen called upon or seized by virtue of the law must obey immediately; he becomes guilty by resisting.

...

10. No-one must be troubled on account of their opinions, even their religious beliefs, provided that their expression does not disturb public order under the law.

11. Free expression of thought and opinions is one of the most precious rights of man. Accordingly, every citizen may speak, write and publish freely, except in order to treat abuses of this freedom in the cases determined by the law.

...

13. General taxation is indispensable to the upkeep of the public force and for all the expenses of government. It should be borne equally by all citizens in proportion to their means.

14. Every citizen has the right, in person or through his representative, to establish the necessity of a tax, freely to consent to it, to follow its usage, and to fix its level, base, collection and duration.

...

17. The right to property being an inviolable and sacred right, no-one may be deprived of it, except when public need, legally established, clearly demands it, and on condition of fair and prior compensation.

FURTHER READING

Doyle, W. 1989. *The Oxford history of the French Revolution*. Oxford: Oxford University Press.
Provides a comprehensive overview of the events of the French Revolution.

Soboul, A. 1989. *The French Revolution 1789–1799: From the storming of the Bastille to Napoléon*. London: Unwin Hyman.
The classic interpretation of the events of the Revolution, still highly regarded.

Sutherland, D. M. G. 1985. *France 1789–1815: Revolution and counter-revolution*. London: Collins.
A scholarly and detailed exploration of the Revolution over a longer historical period, taking account of reaction to the Revolution in early nineteenth-century France.

2

The Revolution of 1848: Republican principles on trial

Nigel Harkness

INTRODUCTION

In the history of France, 1848 is a half-forgotten revolution. It had neither the impact of 1789 in bringing absolute monarchy to an end, nor that of 1870 in firmly embedding Republicanism as the basis of government in France. Instead, it marked a brief transition period between the fall of the constitutional monarchy of **Louis-Philippe** (1830–48) and **Louis-Napoléon**'s *coup d'état* in 1851 which led to the creation of the Second Empire (1852–70). In all, the Second Republic lasted just under four years, making it the shortest-lived of France's five Republics. Nonetheless, it constituted an important reaffirmation and redefinition of the values of 1789, for the revolutionaries of 1848 attempted to found the new Republic on the principles of freedom, justice, democracy and humanitarianism. Their experiment, albeit a failed one, would bring to prominence the positive aspects of the Republican ideal which had been somewhat tarnished by the association of the First Republic with the Terror. Moreover, the actions of two groups, workers and women, and their feminist and socialist interpretations of *liberté, égalité, fraternité*, would pose fundamental ideological questions about Republicanism. In more ways than one, Republican principles were on trial in 1848.

BACKGROUND TO THE REVOLUTION OF 1848

A combination of circumstances was to bring about the revolution of February 1848: economic recession left many unemployed and hungry; there was widespread dissatisfaction with a corrupt and repressive regime; and the middle classes were increasingly frustrated by the fact that, although they wielded considerable economic power, they were excluded from the political process (the right to vote was determined by wealth and property ownership, with the result that the electorate was made up of a privileged and unrepresentative elite).

Opposition to the regime was, however, far from united. Political activism had been stifled by Louis-Philippe's government, and political clubs were illegal, though some did survive as clandestine organizations. Political discussion was confined to two left-wing newspapers, the moderate *Le National* and the more socialist *La Réforme*, but their influence was limited to a small, literate and predominantly urban readership. These restrictions made it difficult for opposition groups to organize. All the same, by early 1848 demands for political change were growing, with properly representative government being seen as a necessary precondition for economic reform.

The opposition movement mobilized support for its cause through a series of banquets. With the freedom to hold meetings severely restricted, these provided a means of organizing opposition under a banner of respectability and legitimacy, because admission was restricted to men who could afford to pay the ticket price, so these were not public meetings. Between July and December 1847, largely middle-class audiences listened to speeches and joined in toasts condemning the government and calling for constitutional reform. Because of the relatively high price of tickets, few workers participated in these banquets.

However, in early 1848 a group of workers and members of the Paris National Guard, the citizen's militia formed during the 1789 Revolution, began to organize a banquet to take place in a working-class district of Paris. This was banned by the government, which was becoming increasingly concerned by such challenges to its legitimacy. Another Paris banquet was arranged for 22 February, but this too was proclaimed illegal. Protest demonstrations were organized, and workers, students and members of the National Guard took to the streets on the day of the planned banquet calling for political reform and the resignation of the Prime Minister, **Guizot**. Unable to count on the loyalty of the National Guard or the regular army, many of whose members were either actively involved in the protests or sympathized with the demands of the protesters, the King's hold on power was severely compromised. Guizot resigned on 23 February.

The crowds greeted this news with joy, but it was soon overshadowed by events outside the Foreign Ministry. Here soldiers shot at the crowd which had gathered and killed 40 or 50 protesters. This incident sparked widespread protest and strengthened the revolutionary will of the masses. Barricades went up throughout Paris and the following day the King's residence, the Tuileries Palace, was attacked. Unable to quash the uprising, Louis-Philippe abdicated in favour of his grandson. But it was too late to save the constitutional monarchy: faced with the revolutionary will of the people, the leaders of the political opposition were preparing to proclaim a Republic.

On the evening of 24 February a provisional government was formed at the Hôtel de Ville. It made a proclamation, signed by 11 men. Among these were the moderate Republicans **Lamartine, Ledru-Rollin, Garnier-Pagès** and **Arago**; the editors of the opposition newspapers *Le National* and *La Réforme*; and **Louis Blanc**, a more radical Socialist.

The proclamation of 24 February did not institute a Republic. In open revolt against the principles of the previous regime, these men held firm to democratic values and called on the people to choose a new national government: 'The Provisional Government wishes to see the Republic established, subject to ratification by the people, who will be consulted immediately.' The language used is measured, and affirms the primacy of the will of the people. It also shows how this nascent Republican government was concerned to satisfy both the conservative forces which could topple it and the people whose desire for social and economic reform had brought them onto the streets. By expressing the desire for a Republic, the Provisional Government responded to the demands of the crowds outside the Hôtel de Ville, who were shouting 'Long live the Republic'. On the other hand, by making the Republic conditional on the democratically expressed will of the people, they also reassured conservatives of their commitment to legitimacy and order. Crucially, this proclamation also highlights the moderate and radical tendencies *within* the heterogeneous grouping that was the Provisional Government. The tension between these tendencies would fundamentally weaken the Republic's capacity for decisive action and strong leadership.

THE PROVISIONAL GOVERNMENT AND REPUBLICAN VALUES

Establishing democracy

The actions of the Provisional Government demonstrate the principles which motivated these men and their vision of the Republic. One of its first acts was to proclaim the abolition of the death penalty for political offences. This measure reaffirmed the democratic values of the nascent Republic (the proclamation cites the fact that 'no cry for revenge or death has come from the mouths of the people' as one of the reasons for this decision), distanced the Provisional Government from the Terror of the 1790s, and reassured those associated with the former regime that none of their leaders would be executed.

Restrictions on freedoms of association and expression were also abolished, leading to the formation of a number of political clubs and newspapers. On 27 April, the government abolished slavery. This had previously been abolished in 1794, but was re-introduced by **Napoléon Bonaparte** in 1802. This abolition of 1848 eliminated one of the last forms of forced servitude. Finally, the government decreed that, for the forthcoming Assembly elections, 'suffrage would be direct, universal, without any property qualification' and that 'all Frenchmen aged twenty-one years or more shall be electors'. This extended democracy further than had previously been the case in France: after the 1789 Revolution, property qualifications had been used to exclude about one-third of the potential electorate. However, the description of this system as one of 'universal' suffrage was called into question by feminist groups: women were still wholly excluded from voting.

The Provisional Government was also advanced in its social thinking. The Education Minister, **Carnot**, presented a bill to the Assembly in June 1848 which proposed a secular education system, with primary education to be universal, free and obligatory. The bill was defeated: conservatives in the Assembly feared that the teachers would be committed Republicans who would spread their ideas to all the villages and towns of France, thus ensuring support for the Republic. The Catholic Church and its political allies were insistent that it should retain its control of education. Carnot's bill was shelved, but it shows the Republicans' belief in the importance of education for establishing a democratic, socially progressive and egalitarian regime. This belief has remained a central one in French Republican thought.

Leftist or Centrist Republicanism?

As already stated, the Provisional Government was a mixed grouping of moderate Republicans and radical Socialists. Socialists wanted the Republic of 1848 to enact significant social and economic reforms which would improve the conditions of the workers, whose protests had been decisive in bringing down Louis-Philippe in the events of February. With unemployment rising, the main demand of the urban proletariat was for work. This was recognized in a proclamation of 25 February: 'The provisional government of the French Republic undertakes to guarantee the workers' livelihood through work. It undertakes to guarantee work for every citizen.' Louis Blanc was the main figure on the Socialist wing of government of 1848. He advocated the formation of workers' cooperatives to take control of and run factories. Such a measure would have signalled an attack on private ownership, and was unacceptable to moderates in the government as well as to the conservative opposition. A compromise was reached with the creation of *Ateliers Nationaux* (national workshops). These were to organize public works for unemployed male workers. In March 1848 approximately 14,000 workers were enrolled in these workshops and by June 1848 this had risen to almost 100,000. But the government was unsuccessful in securing enough large projects for the workshops: nationalization of the railways would have provided such a project, but no agreement could be reached with the railway companies. Increasingly, the workshops became simply a means of distributing a dole to the unemployed.

There was a further compromise between moderates and Socialists in the

Provisional Government over the establishment of the *Commission du Gouvernement pour les Travailleurs* (Government Commission for Workers). This body came to be known as the *Commission du Luxembourg* because it met in the Luxemburg Palace (a highly symbolic location, which had been the meeting place of the *Chambre des Pairs*, the equivalent of the House of Lords in the United Kingdom). The Commission, under the presidency of Louis Blanc, provided a forum for discussing workers' rights, without implicating the government in any demands or proposals which might be labelled 'socialist'. The Commission had no real power, but it did influence two key government decisions regarding workers' rights. On 2 March the Provisional Government issued a decree limiting the working day to ten hours in Paris (11 in the provinces) and abolishing the practice of sub-contracting of work. The long working day was considered to be 'an insult to human dignity', while sub-contracting was described as 'contrary to the ideals of fraternity': the sub-contractor agreed to undertake a particular task for a set sum, then hired labour cheaply by encouraging workers to compete with each other for work, undercutting each other's rates.

As with the Proclamation of the Provisional Government, the language used is significant. Measures which might be considered 'socialist' are justified by Republican values: while this was the first French Republic to be influenced by recognizably socialist thought, it was careful to downplay this in the face of moderate, bourgeois and conservative opposition.

THE SUPREMACY OF THE PEOPLE: THE MARCH 1848 ELECTIONS

Above all, the Provisional Government desired the 'sanction of the people' for the Republic. But this was by no means guaranteed, given that the majority of the electorate was outside Paris, and hence distant from the revolutionary fervour that had swept the capital. Organizing elections based on universal male suffrage was a huge administrative task, and this prevented the Provisional Government from having an early election which would have capitalized on the initial euphoria that greeted the fall of the July Monarchy, and on the disarray of the opposition parties.

The earliest possible date for elections was April. But, as time went on and the opposition began to reorganize, there were demands from left-wing groups for the elections to be postponed. They were concerned about the anti-Republican influence the Church and local landowners would exert on illiterate rural voters, and by the perceived need to educate the people politically, and thus enable them to make an informed democratic choice. It was agreed to postpone the elections from 9 to 23 April, for practical as much as political reasons.

To ensure that the elections would be free and fair, the administrative machine of the previous regime was dismantled. Prefects and Sub-Prefects in each department were dismissed, and replaced by revolutionary *commissaires* (commissioners). The main duty of these officials was to oversee the logistics of the elections in each department, but they, along with primary school teachers, were also instructed to campaign for Republican candidates, and to combat the influence of anti-Republican notables. The effectiveness of such measures was probably limited: many *commissaires* were new to their area and lacked local support; some were standing as candidates themselves; some were opposed on principle to influencing the electorate; and school teachers in general exerted less influence than the local priest. Moreover, the economic decisions taken by Republican leaders further alienated the peasantry, already traditionally hostile to the towns: to avoid bankruptcy, the Provisional Government had raised the main direct tax, the land tax, by 45 centimes. This affected rural France in particular, especially those with small-holdings who already struggled to make a living.

So it is hardly surprising that the elections were not an overwhelming success for the Provisional Government, except in the area of electoral turnout (84 per cent). It is difficult to determine with any certainty what the political make-up of the new assembly was, since there were no organized political parties, and most candidates campaigned as Republicans. Traditionally the election has been viewed as a victory for moderate Republicans (500 seats, as opposed to 100–150 for the radical/socialist Republicans and 250–300 for the right-wing parties). However, given the fact that moderate Republicans were generally unable to control voting in the Assembly, and that only 300 representatives were Republicans before 1848, these figures need to be treated with some caution. They can be set against other estimates of political strength which suggest that the moderate Republicans had 275 seats, the radical/socialist Republicans 75, and the remaining 550 representatives were right-wing former monarchists, who gave pragmatic support to the moderate Republican government.

And so, on 4 May 1848 at the first sitting of the new Assembly, the Republic was officially proclaimed, first by a unanimous vote in the chamber, and then publicly on the steps of the Assembly. This act founded the Republic on democratic legitimacy, rather than revolutionary insurgency, and would condition reactions to future popular uprisings.

Given that the election results were not an overwhelming endorsement of the Republican parties, many argued that the election should either have been called immediately after the February revolution, or postponed for a number of months (see, for instance, de Tocqueville's analysis in the extract at the end of this chapter). But there is evidence to suggest that further delay might have harmed rather than helped the Republican cause, for monarchist forces regrouped and the economic downturn worsened as the year went on. With hindsight, there is no doubt that the Republicans did not do enough to win over rural France.

THE JUNE DAYS

The Provisional Government was constantly trying to negotiate a middle way between moderate and radical elements. Moderate Republicans shared the same concern as the middle classes for stability, democracy and property; the radicals' sympathies lay with the working classes. Hostility between these two classes grew between February and June 1848, when it finally exploded into what **Karl Marx** described as 'the first great battle between the two classes that divide modern society'. The people had expected much of the new Republican government, but economic conditions continued to worsen. Unemployment rose, and the National Workshops offered only a meagre wage. Workers' demonstrations became more frequent as the dispossessed united again against the wealthier classes; this heightened the fear of the revolutionary potential of the masses harboured by the better-off.

It was this fear that drove the conservative Assembly to demand the closure of the National Workshops, which they regarded as both wasteful and potential arenas for fomenting revolution. The Executive Commission (which had succeeded the Provisional Government) was forced to cede to this pressure, and on 22 June the National Workshops were effectively dissolved: workers under 25 years of age were to be conscripted into the army, and the others were to be sent to the provinces. The working classes had just seen their one gain from the February revolution taken away from them.

The reaction of the workers was a spontaneous one – they took to the streets, erected barricades in the poorer areas of Paris and by 23 June much of working-class Paris was in open revolt against the government. Although this was an economic rather than a political rebellion, many considered it an attack on the legitimacy of a democratically elected government. This helps to explain the Assembly's hostility towards the workers' actions, and the ferocity with which the revolt was put down. The restoration of order was entrusted to General **Cavaignac**, who used the army and the National Guard to defeat the rebels. There were battles in Paris from 23 to 25 June, but by 26 June the uprising had been quashed and some 15,000 rebels arrested. The death toll stood at over 2,000. Cavaignac was credited with restoring order, and he was subsequently confirmed by the Assembly as Head of State in order to defend social and political order. This was the first move in a series which fundamentally weakened the Republic. At the same time, the five members of the Executive Commission, who had also been members of the Provisional Government, resigned (among them Lamartine, Arago, Ledru-Rollin and Garnier-Pagès).

THE TRIUMPH OF ORDER: THE DEATH OF THE REPUBLIC

Order was rapidly restored after the June Days, and with it came political repression. The Assembly voted in new measures restricting press freedom and curtailing the activities of political clubs. While the country notionally remained a Republic, the Head of State was an army general, and conservative forces controlled the Assembly. Bourgeois concepts of 'property', 'family' and 'order' gained ground against Republican values. This was reflected in the Constitution of the Second Republic, adopted on 4 November 1848. The preamble stated that the Republic 'has as its basis the Family, Work, Property and Public Order'. Crucially, the Constitution also provided for a directly elected president.

Waiting in the wings was the figure of **Louis-Napoléon**, the nephew of **Napoléon Bonaparte**. He had been elected to the Assembly in September 1848, and stood in the presidential elections of December. His name had a high 'recognition factor' across the country because of his illustrious uncle, and was associated with military glory, authority and order. He won with a comfortable majority, gaining almost three times as many votes as his opponents combined. Under Louis-Napoléon's presidency, the Republic became increasingly conservative: his government contained no Republicans but a number of Royalist notables.

Elections in June 1849 and March 1850 returned a larger number of radical left-wing politicians than in 1848. In response, the Assembly modified the electoral law to reduce the number of those entitled to vote: a residency requirement of three years in the electoral district was introduced, disenfranchising three million electors (out of a total of nine million). The effects of this were more acute in major urban centres with a large migrant population: in Paris 62 per cent of the electorate were excluded by this measure. This spot-reduction of the electorate reduced the electoral support for political radicals, whose power base was mainly in the cities.

Louis-Napoléon soon tried to change the Constitution of the Second Republic to allow him to be re-elected president for a second term of office. This constitutional amendment was passed by the Assembly in July 1851, but not with the necessary two-thirds majority. Louis-Napoléon seized power in a *coup d'état* on 2 December 1851 and declared a presidential regime, a move which encountered some Republican resistance, but which was subsequently ratified by a plebiscite of the people. Seven million electors voted in favour of this move, though there was a high abstention rate, and when these elections took place there were no opposition newspapers, and opposition leaders were either in exile or silent.

A year later, Louis-Napoléon declared his desire to see the re-establishment of France as an Empire, a move which was similarly endorsed in a plebiscite of 20 November in which almost eight million voters supported the proposal. With the proclamation of the Second Empire on 2 December 1852, the Second Republic officially came to an end. But the origins of the Republic's demise can be traced back to June 1848 when, at the first signs of disorder and opposition, the democratically elected assembly gave over leadership to one powerful man, echoing the Directorate's moves of the late 1790s. In 1848 France still seemed unready to sustain a Republican model of government.

WOMEN EXCLUDED FROM THE REPUBLICAN FRATERNITY

Republicanism confronted both socialism and feminism in 1848, and showed itself incapable of assimilating the demands of either group. Like the working classes, women – or at least a group of politically active Parisian women – looked to the Republic to address the injustices from which they suffered: the Napoléonic Code of 1804 deprived them of many legal rights and placed them under the tutelage of either a husband or a father; the abolition of divorce also made them prisoners of marriage. They demanded equality in marriage, the recognition of women as autonomous individuals (that is, not dependent on men) and the right to work, to participate in political activities and to vote. These demands were articulated most vociferously by the newspaper *La Voix des Femmes*, founded in March 1848. This was one of a range of feminist newspapers and clubs which were established when restrictions on political activity were eased in the wake of the February revolution.

A notable feature of the feminist movement of 1848 was the way in which it used the language of Republicanism to advance its cause. Since women were less able to take to the streets in direct action to defend their rights than, for instance, the working classes, their struggle was waged through the printed and spoken word. Here they affirmed their allegiance to the principles which even moderate Republicans espoused, but used these to challenge the blind spots of Republicanism. One of the best examples of this is the interpretation of 'universal suffrage' which the Provisional Government had decreed on 4 March. On 22 March, a delegation of women went to see the Mayor of Paris, to seek clarification on whether this applied to women. Since the government had proclaimed 'universal' suffrage and had abolished all privileges, they argued that logically this meant that women should be able to vote. For the Republican principles of liberty, equality and fraternity would dictate that women were equal to men before the law and should have the right to vote. The 27 March edition of *La Voix des Femmes* reinforced this view (see the second extract at the end of this chapter). Women also sought to align themselves with other oppressed groups, and a number of analogies were drawn between women's condition and that of slaves. On 23 April 1848 *La Voix des Femmes* argued that a woman was subjected to three types of slavery: in her family where she was denied control over her own fate (arranged marriages were still common at this time, and women were rarely consulted on the choice of husband); in society where she was subject to a range of prejudices; and in marriage where she was denied her freedom. Such rhetoric was not new, but it gained increased resonance in April 1848 when the Provisional Government abolished slavery in the colonies.

However, women's demands received little support from the Republican leadership. In the political repression which followed June 1848, *La Voix des Femmes* was closed down, as women's demands were increasingly seen as contrary to the notions of property and family, the two pillars of bourgeois order. Women's exclusion from any nascent Republican fraternity was sealed with the Constitution of November 1848, which affirmed that a woman's civic duty was the care of her family. The Republic did not want women as free and equal sisters, but as wives, mothers and daughters, under the tutelage of a husband or father.

The feminism of 1848 was not a unified movement, and, just like Republicanism itself, was split between moderate and radical tendencies (the latter largely grouped around the clubs and newspapers associated with *La Voix des Femmes*). Among the former, the names of **George Sand** and **Marie d'Agoult** (pseudonym Daniel Stern) stand out. Both women were politically active in 1848: Sand worked closely with Ledru-Rollin, the Minister of the Interior, wrote for the official *Bulletin de la République* and edited her own newspaper *La Cause du Peuple* which, as the title suggests, argued strongly for a socialist Republic; d'Agoult was less directly engaged than Sand (and less socialist in her convictions), but she organized a regular *salon* which was frequented by Republican leaders such as Lamartine, and became a forum for Republican debate. Sand and d'Agoult can be described as moderate feminists since they put Republican principles above their feminist sympathies, and this was most evident in their lack of support for women's suffrage. Both were of the opinion that women's right to vote would come as a natural consequence of Republican reform, but believed that there were more immediate priorities (for instance, ensuring that Republican candidates were returned in the April election), and that demands for women's suffrage at this stage risked alienating moderate Republican support for women's causes.

Feminist activity declined substantially after June 1848. Sand had already withdrawn from politics in May 1848, disillusioned by the conservative nature of the Assembly, while d'Agoult remained as an interested observer of events (she would later write a three-volume history of the Revolution). Although short-lived, the feminist movement of 1848 was advanced in both its thinking and organization, and it continued the work of **Olympe de Gouges** in seeking to affirm the place of women's rights within the rhetoric of Republican universalism. Their ultimate failure simply confirmed the Republic as a masculine concept whose fraternity excluded the 'sisters'.

CONCLUSION

The events and debates of 1848 raise a number of important issues for the notion of a Republican identity. What, if anything, did it mean to be a 'Republican' in 1848? The leaders of the Provisional Government were clearly committed to a programme which would tackle social and economic injustices. However, the use of the designation 'Republican' by representatives of the July Monarchy and by men like Louis-Napoléon rendered the term almost meaningless, and certainly emptied it of all egalitarian or socialist content. By June 1848 the Republic had become little more than a non-monarchical form of government with elections based on universal male suffrage. In many other ways, the Second Republic was as repressive and reactionary as both the regime it had replaced and the dictatorship of the Second Empire which followed it. Nevertheless, the memory of this failed Republican experiment would be crucial in the establishment of the Third Republic, which was not only founded on the same principles of freedom, justice, democracy and humanitarianism as its predecessor, but also learned from the latter's mistakes (notably in its definition of the power accorded to the head of state). Such is the positive legacy of 1848 in the French political tradition.

Extract 2.1: Alexis de Tocqueville, a conservative critic of the 1848 revolution, presents his views on the role played by elections in undermining the Republic

Il y a eu des révolutionnaires plus méchants que ceux de 1848, mais je ne pense pas qu'il y en ait jamais eu de plus sots; ils ne surent ni se servir du suffrage universel, ni s'en passer. S'ils avaient fait les élections le lendemain du 24 février, alors que les hautes classes étaient étourdies du coup qu'elles venaient de recevoir, et quand le peuple était plutôt étonné que mécontent, ils auraient obtenu peut-être une assemblée suivant leur cœur; s'ils avaient hardiment saisi la dictature, ils auraient pu la tenir quelque temps dans leurs mains. Mais ils se livrèrent à la nation et, en même temps, ils firent tout ce qui était le plus propre à l'éloigner d'eux; ils la menacèrent en se livrant à elle; ils l'effrayèrent par la hardiesse de leurs projets et par la violence de leur langage, et l'invitèrent à la résistance par la mollesse de leurs actes; ils se donnèrent les airs d'être ses précepteurs en même temps qu'ils se mettaient dans sa dépendance. Au lieu d'ouvrir leurs rangs après la victoire, il les resserrèrent jalousement, et semblèrent, en un mot, s'être donné à tâche de résoudre ce problème insoluble, à savoir: de gouverner par la majorité, mais contre le goût de celle-ci.

Suivant les exemples du passé sans les comprendre, ils s'imaginèrent niaisement qu'il suffisait d'appeler la foule à la vie politique pour l'attacher à leur cause, et que pour faire aimer la république, c'était assez de donner des droits sans procurer des profits; ils oubliaient que leurs devanciers, en même temps qu'ils rendaient tous les paysans électeurs, détruisaient la dîme, proscrivaient la corvée, abolissaient les autres privilèges seigneuriaux et partageaient entre les anciens serfs les biens des anciens nobles, tandis qu'eux ne pouvaient rien faire de pareil. En établissant le vote universel ils croyaient appeler le peuple au secours de la révolution, ils lui donnèrent seulement des armes contre elle.

Source: Alexis de Tocqueville, 1893: *Souvenirs*. Paris: Calmann Lévy, pp. 145–6

There have been more vicious revolutionaries than those of 1848, but I do not think there have ever been any more foolish; they knew neither how to use universal suffrage, nor how to do without it. Had they held the elections straight after 24 February, while the upper classes were still reeling from the blow they had just received, and the populace was astonished rather than dissatisfied, they might perhaps have obtained an assembly such as they desired; if they had boldly seized dictatorship, they could have held on to it for a time. But they surrendered themselves to the nation and, at the same time, they did everything most likely to distance the nation from them; they threatened it as they put themselves in its hands; they terrified it by the boldness of their projects and their intemperate language, and induced it to resist by the feebleness of their actions; they made themselves out to be its tutors at the same time as they made themselves dependent on it. Instead of opening up after victory, they closed ranks jealously, and seemed, in a word, to have set themselves the task of resolving the irresolvable, that is: to govern by majority rule, but not to the majority's taste.

Following the examples of the past without understanding them, they stupidly imagined that they only had to involve the masses in political life to have their support, and that to forge love for the Republic it was enough to accord rights without procuring any benefits; they were forgetting that those who had gone before them had made the peasantry part of the electorate at the same time as they abolished tithes, banned tied labour, destroyed the other feudal privileges and shared among the former serfs the goods of the former nobles. They, on the other hand, could do nothing similar. By establishing universal suffrage they thought they could call the people to the aid of the Republic, but they simply armed them against her.

Extract 2.2: Feminist comment from the newspaper *La Voix des Femmes*, 1848

La France est en République.

La République, c'est la régénération de la société, la société ce sont les hommes et les femmes. Le plus profond principe de la régénération proclamée par la République c'est l'Égalité, l'Égalité sociale; l'Égalité de tous les membres de la société.

Dire aux femmes: vous n'êtes pas électeurs, vous n'êtes pas éligibles
. . ., c'est refuser d'établir l'Égalité tout en la proclamant, – c'est
déshonorer une victoire remportée pour le bien de tous, – c'est
monopoliser indignement les résultats publics et communs du triomphe,
– c'est n'être plus républicains, – tranchons le mot, c'est être *Aristocrates!*
que la nation lise, réfléchisse et décide.

Source: *La Voix des Femmes*, 27 March 1848

France is now a Republic.

The Republic stands for the regeneration of society, and society is
made up of men and women. The most fundamental principle of the
regeneration proclaimed by the Republic is Equality, Social Equality; the
Equality of all members of society.

To say to women: you are not part of the electorate, you are not
eligible . . ., is to refuse to establish Equality at the same time as
proclaiming it, – it is to dishonour a victory won for the good of all, – it
is to monopolize unworthily the public and common results of the
triumph, – it is to be republican no longer, – let's not beat about the bush,
it is to be *aristocratic!* May the nation read, reflect and decide.

FURTHER READING

Agulhon, M. 1992a. *1848 ou l'apprentissage de la République*, 2nd edn. Paris:
Seuil.
The most detailed overview and analysis of the Second Republic. Also
available in English under the title *The Republican experiment, 1848–1852*.
Cambridge: Cambridge University Press, 1983.
Agulhon, M. 1992b. *Les quarante-huitards*, 2nd edn. Paris: Gallimard.
A collection of documents from 1848 including newspaper articles,
eyewitness accounts, literary extracts and political tracts.
Gemie, S. 1999. *French Revolutions 1815–1914*. Edinburgh: Edinburgh
University Press.
A student-orientated history of the period, with useful accounts of the
philosophical roots of socialism in 1848, and the impact of the 1848
revolution on the provinces. See particularly Chapters 5–8.
Moses, C. G. 1984. *French feminism in the nineteenth century*. New York:
State University of New York Press.
Chapter 6 gives a thorough account of feminist activity from 1848 to 1851.
Website: Pamphlets and periodicals of the French Revolution of 1848.
http://humanities.uchicago.edu/orgs/ARTFL/projects/CRL/.
Contains a searchable database of digitized documents (newspapers,
political tracts, pamphlets) from 1848 to 1851.

3

The Paris Commune of 1871: the Red Republic's triumph and defeat

Rachael Langford

INTRODUCTION

In March 1871, the city of Paris rose up in opposition to the national government. Watched by the occupying Prussian army which encircled Paris, the city ran itself almost as a state within a state – the 'Paris Commune' – for two and half months. But, on 21 May, government troops breached Paris's defences and poured in. A week of ferociously bloody government repression followed, and those involved with the Commune, the 'Communards', were executed, deported, or condemned to other penalties in a series of military trials which continued for several years. Thus between 1871 and 1880, when the Republic was being established on a durable footing in France, radical left-wing Republicanism was largely absent from the public arena because of the death, imprisonment or exile of so many involved in the Commune.

The Paris Commune rocked France to its core. In the provinces of France, Paris was seen as having once again brought shame and chaos to the country. The words of pundits, politicians and public figures of the day show that a desperate thirst for vengeance against the Commune's 'crimes' mobilized France in the early years of the Third Republic. Indeed, the Paris Commune represents both a paradox and a turning point in French Republicanism. Strains of socialist Republicanism triumphed, albeit briefly, in this last of France's nineteenth-century revolutions, and yet the defeat of the Commune consecrated conservative and moderate Republicanism – the Republicanism of the bourgeoisie – as the only acceptable face of Republican government.

BACKGROUND

The Franco-Prussian War

From the mid-nineteenth century onwards, Prussia had developed into a formidable political and military presence in Europe, defeating and annexing or forming alliances with weaker states around it. The leaders of late nineteenth-century Prussia, particularly the Prussian Chancellor **Otto von Bismarck**, dreamed of creating a united, powerful Germany, which would rival France and Britain in importance on the world stage. France saw Prussia's expansion as a threat, but did not have any real understanding of how far Prussia had progressed militarily and politically. Prussians were still seen in the popular press as laughable characters, uncivilized and jovial.

In early July 1870, a question over succession to the Spanish throne arose, and Prussia put forward a candidate from the Prussian royal house. France objected at once, requesting not only that the candidate be withdrawn, but also that Prussia should never renew such a claim to the throne. Prussia withdrew the candidature, but refused to make promises for the future. And so, on 15 July 1870, France declared war on Prussia. There is no doubt that France was somewhat provoked into this declaration of war, which served Prussian ambitions well. It was still foolhardy on France's part, and it belied a terrible underestimation of the military and strategic power of the modernized Prussia. The war was an unmitigated disaster for France. In just six weeks, Emperor **Louis-Napoléon III** was reduced to surrendering to the Prussians. With his surrender, the Second Empire collapsed.

Defeat gave France's collective conscience an enormous battering, for defeat had simply never been envisaged, still less the total collapse of the ruling regime. Second Empire France had been full of confidence in its international standing. Parisians, in particular, considered themselves to be among the most cultured people on earth. This self-confidence of Second Empire France made the feeling of horror and incomprehension in the face of military defeat and political collapse all the more acute.

Formal confirmation of Napoléon III's surrender to Prussia reached Paris on 3 September, and Republicans of all persuasions came onto the streets of the city calling for a Republic to be declared. Swept along by the crowds, the Republican deputies of Paris met at the Hôtel de Ville on 4 September, and the Republic was duly announced. There was a semblance of election to government. The Republican deputies of Paris and prominent left-wing Republicans who had also crowded into the Hôtel de Ville were selected according to the acclamation of the assembled crowds. Government posts were filled, in a somewhat haphazard manner.

The new government termed itself the Government of National Defence, and its first task was to attend to the war with Prussia. At first the government thought Prussia would not want to continue with the war now that the political regime with which it had been in conflict had gone. However, the Prussians made it clear that they would only settle for peace terms that ceded to them the resource-rich French territories of Alsace and Lorraine. Such terms showed the Republicans that the war was against France, not the Second Empire, and because the Republic was now in charge this war was now also a war against the Republic.

The siege of Paris

The Emperor had surrendered and the regime had collapsed, but people on the streets of Paris were adamant that the war should continue. Defeat was put down to incompetent imperial leadership, a lack of real patriotism, and a kind of moral decadence. Most people believed that the new Republic would bring honour back to France. In the meantime, Prussian troops advanced inexorably on Paris, and the city was fully encircled by them on 20 September 1870. Four months of siege began for Paris. Throughout these months, French sorties, retreats, and defeats accumulated. The winter of 1870–1871 was a harsh one, and the new Republican government did not ration food and fuel in the face of a potentially protracted siege. This meant that those in the besieged city who could afford extortionate prices for food and fuel as stocks became scarce did so, and that those who could not starved and froze. Paris under siege became in effect two cities. Child mortality and death rates for the elderly and infirm among the poorest sectors of the population grew to four times what they had been the preceding winter.

This situation led to the development of a separate political consciousness among the least favoured Parisians. All Parisians felt themselves cut off from the rest of France by the siege, but the poorest also felt cut off from their better-off fellows in the city, and from the Republicans in power who seemed keen to protect their own bourgeois interests, rather than ease the welfare of those suffering most in the siege. Mutual scorn between the different social classes resident in Paris developed, and from October onwards there were several incidents of insurrection against the Government of National Defence.

As early 1871 dawned, French military defeats continued, and, with every military failure, the moderate Republican Government of National Defence lost prestige. Eventually on 20 January a final attempt was made to find a way out of the blockade, pitting French volunteers and regulars against the Prussian forces to the west of Paris. The result was another French disaster, with troops shooting into their own lines by mistake, and others fleeing from the battle back into Paris. The day after this rout, the Government of National Defence reluctantly accepted that it had to capitulate to Prussia and seek an armistice.

The terms of the armistice were harsh for the French. Cessation of fighting was granted until 19 February, to allow France to go to the polls to elect an Assembly that would have the authority to negotiate for peace or to continue with war. In the meantime, Paris was to pay a huge war indemnity. Further, the

French army was to surrender all its arms and colours, save for one regular division of infantry which would be left armed in case of internal rebellion. The French government pleaded that the Paris National Guard (see below) be left armed, for any attempt at disarming them was sure to result in armed resistance by the rebellious Guards. Already feverish politically, Paris's temperature rose further at the news of the capitulation. This humiliating armistice, reached after all the hardships of the siege had been borne with fortitude, seemed a betrayal of all that the French Republic should stand for.

THE DECLARATION OF THE COMMUNE

The elections agreed by the terms of the armistice took place on 8 February. A very conservative majority was returned: France outside Paris saw the Second Empire as having started the war and the Republic as having lost it. Unsurprisingly, therefore, provincial France looked back to what seemed the only remaining legitimate political tradition – that of the ultra-conservative monarchists – and voted accordingly. But left-wing Republican Parisians were horrified. They felt that they had endured alone the extreme hardships of the last months of the war, only to find themselves dictated to by an Assembly of conservative country squires prepared to accept Prussia's crippling peace terms. Moreover, they felt that they had been cheated out of the true Republic, for the possibility of a 'Red' Republic of social and economic equality had receded once more. It was replaced by a contradiction of a regime, a Republic that was extremely conservative and pro-monarchy in principle.

Heading the new Assembly as President of the Republic was **Adolphe Thiers**. Thiers and the Assembly wasted no time in cementing their unpopularity with the people of Paris. They accepted Bismarck's terms for permanent peace, ceding all of Alsace and most of Lorraine, agreeing to pay a huge war indemnity, and allowing the conquering Prussians a victory parade through Paris. They embarked on legislation enforcing the immediate payment of debts and rents, suspended for the duration of the war. They also ended the pay of the volunteer citizen militia, the National Guard. This pay included allowances for dependent wives and children, and had acted as a kind of unemployment benefit during the war when many had been unable to work.

These measures hit the working class of Paris hard, but they also hit at the petty bourgeoisie. Shopkeepers, artisans, and lowly clerks rarely owned their own premises and homes, and most had been unable to earn a normal living during the war and siege and had relied on the daily pay of the National Guard to keep their heads above water through the economic stagnation of the war. By forcing payment of rent and debts and ending the National Guards' pay, Thiers and the Assembly united whole swathes of Parisians who would not otherwise have had common cause.

The National Guard

The Paris National Guard was the citizen militia which had existed since the Revolution of 1789. It was expanded during the summer of 1870 in response to the need to protect Paris from the Prussian advance. With this expansion, many recruits from lower down on the social ladder, who had radical Republican sympathies, had been incorporated into its ranks.

There were two decisive characteristics to the National Guard. First, it was a locally recruited force: battalions were raised neighbourhood by neighbourhood, reflecting the social and political make-up of the district from which they came. Second, each battalion elected its own commanders. In radical districts, well-known political speakers and activists from the area became officers, while bourgeois districts elected their local notables and men of substance. In conviction and composition, the Paris National Guard reflected the state of Paris in 1871 as a thoroughly divided city. To use the terms of Thiers' Republican government, the west and south districts raised 'good' (i.e. moderate or conservative) battalions, and to the east and north were the 'bad' (i.e. radical) battalions.

During the months of the siege, there had been almost no economic activity, and without the meagre Guards' pay many families would not have survived. Tours of sentry duty and patrols of the Paris fortifications took up some of the Guards' time. But, with economic activity so stagnant, Guardsmen had much time to spare. Battalion meetings frequently took on the aspect of local welfare societies, social clubs, and political gatherings. Indeed, in some districts, the activities of the National Guard vigilance committees in seeing to the social and welfare needs of their neighbourhood practically took over the role of the local municipal administrations.

The socially and politically engaged spirit of the radical battalions of the Paris National Guard was at the ideological heart of the Paris Commune. There was an overwhelming sense of neighbourhood ownership in all that the radical Guards did. The Republican government seemed not to care about the hardships of the poorer districts under the siege. In contrast, the radical National Guard committees began piecemeal to set up a parallel model of Republicanism within the Republic. They partially enacted the idea of a socially and economically just Republic through their neighbourhood social work, and talked of their radical Republican aspirations in political meetings.

The Guards were used throughout the siege in sorties out of Paris against the Prussians. The Government of National Defence and its army command felt that the Guards were dangerously rebellious and militarily incapable. The Guards themselves simmered with resentment at being badly deployed and commanded in the field, and thus prevented from achieving much. In the divided city, this further dissent over the status of a force which involved the majority of the young male Parisians was another cause for hostility between Paris and the national Republican government. It was from the radical National Guard battalions that the push for the Paris Commune emerged.

18 March 1871

Thiers and the Assembly did not intend to let the unruly Parisians and their armed National Guard continue their challenges to the conservative Republic. On 18 March, just before daybreak, regular army troops made their way up the *Butte Montmartre* (the hill on which the Montmartre district stands) to capture the National Guard cannons gathered there. The regulars met no resistance, and the cannons were secured. This should have been the first success in the government operation to disarm Paris. But there was no way for the regulars to move the cannons off the hill. By some oversight characteristic of French army organization at the time, the company of horses to tow away the guns was missing.

Dawn came and, as the regulars sat with the captured but immobile cannons, the alarm was raised across Montmartre. Men, women and children challenged the soldiers, who fraternized with them, ignoring the commands of their officers to disperse the crowds. There were scuffles, and the regulars at Montmartre, mixed with the crowds, arrested their officers, later shooting two of them. The scenes of fraternization between the army and the people were repeated across Paris. Barricades were thrown up, and the government and army high command, panicked that they had lost control of the situation, evacuated to Versailles where the conservative Assembly joined them two days later. Panicking bourgeois citizens rushed out of Paris too. Paris was suddenly, unexpectedly, in the hands of the Parisians. Municipal elections were held on 26 March, returning a radical majority to the city council. The new city council gave itself the revolutionary title of 'Paris Commune', and was proclaimed to scenes of jubilation in front of the Hôtel de Ville in the spring sunshine of 28 March.

REPUBLICAN VALUES IN THE COMMUNE

The title 'Paris Commune' linked the insurrection of 1871 back to the Revolutionary nationalism of 1792, when the Commune of Paris had seized the reins of power to overthrow the monarchy, defend the nation and silence the enemies of the Revolution. In addition, the title denoted a grass-roots, popular form of Republican local democracy; where Paris was concerned, this meant the right to autonomous local government within the structure of France as a whole. In the Commune's 'Declaration to the French People' of 19 April, it was promised that communes (i.e. local municipalities) all over France would receive equal rights to self-government. This was in line with

Proudhonist (named after the political theorist **Pierre-Joseph Proudhon**) left-wing thought, which gave primacy to the commune, the smallest unit of municipal administration, as the most important unit of political organization. It was in contrast, however, to the mainstream currents of radical French Republicanism which had grown up through the century and was rooted in Jacobinism. Jacobin Republicanism was centralizing in tendency, and advocated firm revolutionary leadership from above, not federative-style democracy organized at a local level. These two left-wing tendencies of Proudhonism and Jacobinism, decentralizing and centralizing, co-existed in the Paris Commune, and led to bitter wrangles on the part of the Commune's leaders over the direction to be taken by the insurrection.

The Commune's most pressing matters were economic and military ones: it needed to find money to keep the city running smoothly and it needed to organize the defence of the city against the Versailles government troops. Most of its debates were therefore given over to these matters. As a form of government, external necessity and internal conflict made it unstable: in the ten weeks of its existence, the administration took three different forms. An executive commission of seven men was set up on 29 March to carry out the Commune's decrees, and under it were various commissions overseeing the different aspects of government. This original executive was replaced on 20 April by another, composed of all the delegates heading the various under-commissions. The latter executive lasted only until 1 May, when it was swept aside by a Committee of Public Safety made up of five men, and whose title harked back to the Committee of Public Safety of the 1790s.

The 1871 Committee of Public Safety was formed following a split in the Commune. The majority (Jacobins and the followers of **Auguste Blanqui**) favoured concentrating power in a central authority, the Committee of Public Safety, in an attempt to reinvigorate the defence of the city against Versailles troops. A minority wished grass-roots, participatory democracy to prevail, however severe the civil war might become. The majority won the debate, and the Committee remained in charge until the end of the Commune, holding its last session a week before the Commune's final defeat. The Commune's minority members saw the Committee as a defeat for the true spirit of 1789 Republicanism. For them, rather than heralding a new, modern epoch of revolutionary self-government by the people for the people, this form of government looked backwards to the traditions of the 1790s, where the people were governed and purged from above for their own benefit.

Despite these internal conflicts and the state of civil war, the Commune did make policies significant to the history of French Republicanism. There was not always the time to carry these policies through to action, but in key areas the Commune was not short of ideas for the reorganization of society. The two main areas in which the Commune has been considered innovative concerned the welfare of women and of workers.

Gender

During the Commune, women spoke publicly about political affairs: there were women's political clubs, and prominent female political speakers and journalists. Many of these were widely known and respected. The most famous was probably **Louise Michel**, who raised the alarm in Montmartre on 18 March, and who was deported to New Caledonia for her part in the Commune. Some pro-Commune women armed themselves, and many were present on the barricades as nurses and *cantinières*. Many others were involved in war work making munitions and uniforms, or replacing ousted nuns from the secularized hospitals and schools. Alongside all these roles, women were also involved in community welfare work.

Commune legislation recognized women's particular concerns in the workplace, while still regarding them as entities apart. The Commune decreed equal pay for teachers of both sexes for the first time ever in France, and it sought to organize women's cooperatives to cover 'women's trades' such as dressmaking and laundry work. It also decided to grant widows' pensions to common-law wives of National Guardsmen, and to give allowances to the children of common-law wives. This was a radical move, but the proofs of morality and stable relationships required were stringent, and cases were still decided by men. A committee including women was appointed to consider the reform of girls' education, and an industrial arts school for girls was opened. The Commune also intended the complete secularization of education for women, until then the province of religious teaching personnel.

The vast majority of nineteenth-century Republicans, moderate, conservative or socialist, did not believe that women had a role in the political domain. Women were housewives, mothers, and, more controversially, workers: they were social entities, but not political citizens like men. So, while the Commune made improvements to women's social situation and accorded them an important support role in the insurrection, it expressed no desire to change their political status. Moreover, this was not part of the demands made by women either. Staunchly Republican women in the *Union des Femmes pour la Défense de Paris et les Soins aux Blessés* (Women's Union for the Defence of Paris and the Care of the Injured), the main women's organization associated with the Commune, did not argue for the extension of voting rights to women and nor did women in the political clubs. As in the First World War, women were valued as social and economic entities, but were far from acceding to formal political rights as citizens.

Yet women are part of the Commune's enduring myth. The presence of politically active women involved alongside men in street combat horrified bourgeois morality across Europe for decades. The legend of the *pétroleuses*, largely fictional woman fire-bombers, was an especially powerful one. Versailles troops took their bloody revenge for the Commune on women as much as on men, for women's involvement in armed insurrection made them women no longer in the eyes of the political Right.

Class

Communards were the people, not the proletariat. In part, this is because there was no large-scale urban industry in Paris at the time: the large factories that did exist were located on the outskirts of the city. The workers of 1871 involved in the Commune were predominantly skilled or semi-skilled, and the Commune did not promote a class-war type of revolution, despite later Marxist readings of its significance. In essence, the Commune believed in the association of producers – the shop-owner and shop assistant, for example – for the economic and social betterment of all, and it was those who earned money idly (landlords and those with inherited wealth) who were scorned. Overall, the Commune's economics were conservative: key government institutions such as the *Banque de France* remained untouched, and ordinary citizens went about their commercial business unimpeded. Although the rhetoric of the political clubs and the radical newspapers was often violent, its targets were not the bourgeoisie as a class but the Republic of 4 September, the Versailles Assembly, Thiers, monarchists and Bonapartists.

Certainly the Commune's worker legislation does not reveal any project for the economic reorganization of society. The Commune urged the setting up of local labour exchanges by *mairies* (district town halls), to replace the expensive private employment agencies. Another reform was made to prevent employers from taking fines (for poor punctuality, for example) directly out of wages. The most significant reform was the suppression of night baking. Bakers were disqualified by law from striking, and night baking was felt to prevent them from spending time with their families and from educating themselves. These reforms to labour practices were not wide-ranging, and responded to long-standing demands on the part of workers.

The Commune's reform which most responded to popular demands was the secularization of society. It may seem paradoxical that so abstract a notion could be a prime demand of ordinary Parisian people, but established religion (rather than individual religious practice) was considered to underpin both monarchism and Bonapartism. It was felt to be obscurantist, to impede progress by keeping the people in the dark, to be anti-scientific (and the late nineteenth century was as much the age of science as ours is of information technology); established religion was considered to be fundamentally anti-Republican. A second, and allied, reform by the Commune had been called for throughout France by popular associations from the 1860s onwards. This was the provision of free, secular state education for all. The Commune had neither the funds nor the time to organize this fully, but its Education Commission deliberated the matter in depth and encouraged *mairies* to secularize their local schools and to provide free education wherever possible.

Therefore, the Commune was not really a radical class war seeking fundamental alterations to economic power relations. This is confirmed by the fact that the Republican governments of 1875 and beyond had no conceptual difficulty incorporating the main tenets of the Commune – secularism and free state primary education for all – into moderate Republican reforms such as the *lois Jules Ferry* (**Jules Ferry** laws), which increasingly secularized French education and society from the 1880s onwards.

CONCLUSION

Defeat and reaction

Unlike the revolutionary movements of 1789 and 1848, the Commune of 1871 did not spark similar uprisings across the country and abroad. Although Communes were declared in a few Republican industrial centres such as St Étienne and Lyon, they lasted only a few days. This lack of similar movements elsewhere suggests that the insurrection responded to particularly Parisian concerns, those produced by the exceptional circumstances of war and siege. Moreover, the Commune lasted a mere two and a half months. Material poverty and military defencelessness beset it. Its leaders spent much time arguing among themselves as to the way forward. It posed no credible long-term threat to the national government, nor to France as a whole. And yet its end heralded frenzied vengeance and a desire for atonement at any cost. Why was this so?

Essentially, the Commune's 'crimes' were threefold. First, its very existence challenged the legitimacy of the Third French Republic which was declared on 4 September 1870. The Commune's existence as a parallel government drew attention to the shaky foundations of this new regime, a Republic which had not been elected in any recognized sense. Second, the Commune gave voice to interpretations of Republicanism which moderate Republicans had fought to sideline since the end of the French Revolution, because they threatened the interests of the comfortably off and were felt to make a Republic politically unpalatable. These unwanted interpretations were those which prioritized the creation of a more socially and economically equal society. Third, the Commune gave a voice to those who had, despite the democratic gains stemming from the Revolution, been largely excluded from political decision-making. Although there were committees and leaders of the Commune, the largest force of opinion was the people. The populace made its feelings known in political clubs, in rallies and demonstrations, and in actions of despair and frustration such as the burning of buildings and the shooting of hostages. Often, decisions were made in response to the demands of the people; the Commune's democracy frequently worked from the bottom up.

'Right-thinking' French people of the time considered these 'crimes' heinous in themselves. In the opinion of these same people, however, it was the historical backdrop to the Commune that magnified these 'crimes' into outrages against all decency. This seizing of power by ordinary Parisians took place in a context of national disaster – the sudden collapse of the previous regime, the loss of the territories of Alsace and Lorraine, the occupation of France by the hated Prussian army. All these heaped ignominy on France, and the Communards' usurpation of political power seemed expressly designed to magnify this humiliation.

The Commune's legacy to Republicanism

The Commune has become significant in French Republicanism less for what it actually was than for what it was taken to be. The defeat of the Commune ensured the survival of the Republic; the country had already veered to the right, as the elections of February 1871 had shown. Had the Commune not been crushed, it seems likely that monarchists would have sought a restoration to the throne; certainly Bismarck suggested that the Prussians would rehabilitate Napoléon III should the Commune not be overthrown. Condemnation and pursuit of the Communards provided an enemy within around which a national consensus could be formed in the early years of the Third Republic. Once the amnesty to exiled Communards had been granted in the 1880s (by which time mainstream Republicans had largely attributed blame for the Commune to the Second Empire and the conservatives), the focus shifted to seeking revenge on the external enemy for the lost territories of Alsace and Lorraine. In the 1880s and 1890s, returnee Communards found political niches across the Republican political spectrum; in the **Boulanger** crisis of the mid-1880s, a brand of radical Republican nationalism attracted a fair share of those who had been active during the Commune.

It could be argued that the Commune's greatest long-term consequences have been in left-wing mythology. Although, as we have seen, the Commune was never a workers' revolution in the way that Marxists have wanted it to be, on its formation in 1921, the *Parti Communiste Français* (French Communist Party) explicitly claimed itself to be reconnecting with the traditions of the Commune. **Marx**, Lenin and Stalin all wrote about the Commune, and its failures were analysed by Communists to provide a model for successful popular revolution.

A lasting effect of the Commune was on the status of Paris within the Republic. The Paris National Guard was disbanded immediately. Self-government for the city under a Mayor of Paris had been granted by the Government of National Defence, and was immediately abolished; Jacques **Chirac**'s election in 1977 to the revived Mayorship made him the first Mayor of Paris since the defeat of the Commune. The National Assembly and the President continued to sit outside the city at Versailles, only returning to Paris in 1879. And the Constitution of 1875 set out to form a Senate which would under-represent the cities of France. All these measures reduced the stature of Paris as the political leader of France, and suspicion of the city and its unruly population continued well into the twentieth century. In a highly symbolic gesture, at the liberation of Paris in 1944 **de Gaulle** refused to appear at the Hôtel de Ville to be acclaimed by the people of Paris. He had no desire for his authority to be seen as legitimated by the people of Paris, that revolutionary people of the preceding two centuries.

Extract 3.1: Maxime du Camp, a conservative critic of the Commune, is overtly hostile to the Communards

Les chefs, à force de vivre sans contrainte, n'ayant les uns et les autres que leur fantaisie pour règle et leurs passions pour guide, en arrivent à dédaigner les notions les plus élémentaires qui régissent les sociétés. Ils ont arboré des devises auxquelles leur façon de vivre et leur mode de penser ont donné un perpétuel démenti. Comment, en effet, faire comprendre à des hommes incultes ou infatués que liberté signifie soumission aux lois ; égalité, participation légale à des droits abstraits ; fraternité, abnégation de soi-même au profit de la communauté ? Bien plus, pour ces gens, liberté signifie le pouvoir de tout faire sans contrôle ; égalité, participation à toutes les jouissances et occupation du premier rang ; fraternité, utilisation de la communauté au profit de soi-même ; c'est le renversement de la proposition ; mais le parti révolutionnaire ne l'a jamais interprétée autrement, et c'est pourquoi il a toujours versé dans la cruauté.

Dans ces temps de surexcitation morbide, les chefs deviennent violents, et s'exaspèrent mutuellement dans leurs discussions confuses ; les soldats se grisent de leur importance, mêlent l'ivresse de l'alcool à celle des doctrines impies et deviennent fous.

Source: Maxime du Camp, 1881: *Les convulsions de Paris*, vol. 4, 'La Commune à l'Hôtel de Ville', Paris: Hachette, pp. 150–1

The leaders, by dint of living without any constraints, and having nothing more than their whims as rules and their passions as a guide, come to despise the most basic notions which regulate societies. They sported mottoes to which their way of life and their way of thinking constantly gave the lie. How, indeed, could one make uneducated or infatuated men understand that liberty means submitting to laws; equality, legal participation in abstract rights; fraternity, sacrificing oneself for the benefit of the community? It is far more the case that, for these people, liberty means the power to do anything without control; equality, participating in all pleasures and being number one; fraternity, using the community for one's own benefit. It's the phrase inverted; but the revolutionary party has never understood the phrase otherwise, and that is why it has always lapsed into cruelty.

In this period of morbid frenzy, the leaders get violent, and infuriate each other in their woolly discussions; the soldiers get drunk with their own importance, become intoxicated by alcohol mixed with ungodly dogmas, and go mad.

Extract 3.2: Louise Michel's words to the court in the Fourth *Conseil de Guerre* (military trial), 1871

J'appartiens toute entière à la Révolution sociale et je déclare accepter la responsabilité entière de mes actes. . . . Vous me reprochez d'avoir participé à l'assassinat de généraux ? A cela, je répondrais oui, si je m'étais trouvée à Montmartre, quand ils ont voulu faire tirer sur le peuple. Je n'aurais pas hésité à faire tirer moi-même sur ceux qui donnaient des ordres semblables. Mais lorsqu'ils ont été prisonniers, je ne comprends pas qu'on les ait fusillés, et je regarde cet acte comme une insigne lâcheté. . . .

On me dit que je suis complice de la Commune. Assurément oui, puisque la Commune voulait avant tout la Révolution sociale et que la Révolution sociale est le plus cher de mes vœux. Bien plus, je me fais honneur d'être l'un de promoteurs de la Commune, qui n'est d'ailleurs pour rien, pour rien, qu'on le sache bien, dans les assassinats et les incendies . . . Voulez-vous connaître les vrais coupables ? Ce sont les gens de la police, et plus tard, peut-être, la lumière se fera sur tous ces événements dont on trouve aujourd'hui tout naturel de rendre responsables tous les partisans de la Révolution sociale. . . .

Vous êtes des hommes qui allez me juger ; vous êtes devant moi à visage découvert, et moi je ne suis qu'une femme, et pourtant je vous regarde en face. Je sais bien que tout ce que je pourrai vous dire ne changera en rien votre sentence.

Source: Jacques Rougerie, 1978: *Procès des Communards*. Paris: Gallimard, pp. 88–9

I belong wholly to the social Revolution and I declare that I fully accept responsibility for all my acts. . . . You criticize me for having taken part in the killing of the generals? To this I would reply yes, if I had been at Montmartre, when they wanted to fire on the people. I would not have hesitated myself to have those who give that kind of order fired on. But when they were prisoners, I don't understand why they were shot, and I consider this act to be a particularly cowardly one. . . .

I'm told that I am complicit with the Commune. Absolutely, since the Commune sought, above all, social Revolution and since social Revolution is the dearest of my wishes. Much more than this, I am proud of being one of the promoters of the Commune, which, moreover, had nothing, nothing whatsoever, to do with the killings and the fires. . . . Do you want to know who was really guilty of this? The police, and perhaps later on light will be shed on all these events which at present everyone finds it quite natural to blame on the supporters of social Revolution. . . .

You are men who are going to sentence me; you are there before me with your faces exposed; you are men, and I am only a woman, and yet I look you in the eye. I know full well that nothing I could say to you would change your sentencing.

FURTHER READING

Horne, A. 1989. *The fall of Paris: the siege and the Commune 1870–71*. London: Macmillan.
  Lively account of the Commune and the siege of Paris. Detailed on events and quotes widely from contemporary sources, but gives a sometimes biased account of the conflict.
Rougerie, J. 1978. *Procès des Communards*. Paris: Gallimard.
  The words of the defeated Communards themselves, from their military trials in the 1870s, with explanatory commentary by Rougerie.
Tombs, R. 1999. *The Paris Commune 1871*. London: Longman.
  A balanced account of the meanings and significance of the Commune, supported by astute assessments of documentary evidence.
Website: North Western University's Special Collection of digitized photographs of the siege and the Commune.
  http://www.library.northwestern.edu/spec/siege/.
  This searchable database contains over 1,200 images of Paris and its inhabitants from 1870 to 1871.

4

The Dreyfus affair of 1894: Republicanism and its challengers

David Hanley

INTRODUCTION

French commentators usually refer to the *affaire* **Dreyfus**, suggesting that it has an importance that goes far beyond that of a mere court case from the closing years of the nineteenth century. With the Dreyfus affair, the existence of the Third Republic itself was briefly called into question and so, more profoundly, was the question of French identity. It may well be true that the *affaire* brought little new to French politics, but it certainly triggered a deep and widespread questioning of what 'France' really meant.

On 22 December 1894, an army officer, Captain Alfred Dreyfus, was sentenced to prison for spying on behalf of Germany. The case attracted little controversy at the time, although some disquiet was felt that the conviction largely rested on a report allegedly in Dreyfus' handwriting. Some Dreyfus sympathizers, such as the novelist **Émile Zola**, suspected a miscarriage of justice; many believed that Dreyfus had been sacrificed because of his Jewish origins. In the course of the next few years, 'Dreyfusard' campaigners began slowly to unravel the truth. Colonel Georges Picquart, an officer in military intelligence, worked in the face of obstruction and threats, and discovered that another intelligence officer had crudely forged additional evidence against Dreyfus. The officer concerned committed suicide, raising the temperature considerably.

The *affaire*'s reverberations began to spread across French society. The army and most senior politicians were anxious to let sleeping dogs lie, and they found support from a range of conservative and nationalist writers, who accused 'Dreyfusard' campaigners of being anti-French troublemakers. But many left-wing writers and politicians supported campaigns for a retrial. Throughout 1899, tension rose as prospects of a retrial loomed. Two Defence

Ministers resigned in an attempt to pressure the government into blocking a retrial. One government fell because the Prime Minister tried to move the case to a court less favourable to revising the original verdict. A farcical, nationalist *coup d'état* was attempted in February; in June, right-wing thugs beat up the President at a racecourse while the police turned a blind eye.

At last the retrial took place, before a military court at Rennes from August to September 1899. Its verdict was again that Dreyfus was guilty, but with extenuating circumstances. This was a classic fudge, and it reflected conflicting pressures from state institutions determined not to lose control, and from politicians desperate to find a way out when faced with strong public opinion and increasingly irrefutable evidence in Dreyfus' favour. Dreyfus was released shortly afterwards but would have to wait until 1904 for a full pardon and restoration of his civil rights. In the meantime, long-standing tensions within French politics and society had been brought to a head.

THE POLITICAL CONTEXT OF THE DREYFUS CASE

The importance of the Dreyfus case lies less in its intrinsic interest (the struggle of one man for justice against a dishonest state machine) than in what it tells us about the politics of Republican France. In the mid- and late 1870s, political conservatives still hoped that the Republic would be short-lived and that the monarchy could be restored. But provincial French voters were increasingly ready to back a moderate Republic that would give them what they wanted: secure property rights, a market economy protected against foreign competition, law and order, and a modest degree of social mobility via the education system. A constitutional crisis in May 1877 had seen the failure of attempts by conservative monarchists led by the President, **Marshal MacMahon,** to dissolve parliament and appoint a monarchist government in defiance of the Republican parliamentary majority elected in 1876. But eventually MacMahon was forced to resign, and Republicans assumed office strengthened by the crisis. By the late 1880s, Republicans had established control of the political system, and a pattern of government soon evolved in which shifting coalitions, formed from loosely structured parliamentary parties dominated by local leaders (*notables*), were the rule. The average life span of a government cabinet was six months, but this apparent volatility concealed a high degree of continuity among the politicians who made up government as well as a clear continuity in policy.

Republican governments did not carry out extensive public policies of the type familiar in Europe today. This is understandable, for mainstream Republicanism was not an ideology of social and economic equality. As preceding chapters have argued, moderate Republicanism supported meritocracy and equality of opportunity, both of which necessarily imply different outcomes for those involved. What the Republicans did seek to do was to implant firmly their idea of democracy, confident that this would enable a reasonable measure of social justice to be realized. They concentrated heavily on reforming the administration, purging non-Republican civil servants and replacing them with ideologically favourable ones. They concentrated too on education: in the Republican world-view the school was a key site of political struggle, for it was the place where the loyalties and ideas of the future citizen were formed. As such, it could not be left to spread rival ideologies associated with the political Right and the restoration of the monarchy.

Much of the Republicans' political effort went into weakening Catholic influence on schooling, for Catholicism tended to be associated with the political Right and the Church had traditionally monopolized primary education across the country. Thus, in the 1880s, the Prime Minister **Jules Ferry** introduced a number of key educational reforms. These instituted free, compulsory and secular education for all children up to the age of 12, and banned members of religious orders from teaching in the State's primary schools. The Jesuits, the major Catholic teaching order, were expelled from France, and other orders had to seek government registration.

By the 1890s then, the Republicans appeared comfortably in control. Elections turned up majorities in their favour. Openly anti-Republican opposition was reduced to a few dozen disorganized deputies elected from the (mainly Catholic) periphery of France. School reform seemed to have guaranteed the primacy of Republican values for the political future. Republicans could even afford the luxury of internal dissension and conflict. Increasingly, Republican politics was becoming polarized between mainstream, moderate Republicans, content to consolidate recent gains, and the Radicals, who wanted to take the democratic and secularist agenda further than their moderate colleagues. In policy terms, Radicals wanted to abolish the Senate (the indirectly elected upper house of parliament) and the President also, and to have certain officials such as magistrates elected. They also advocated the introduction of income tax, an anathema to mainstream Republicans, who believed that individuals should keep what they earned. Most importantly they wanted to separate the Catholic Church from the French State.

This was more than just a symbolic gesture, important though the symbolism was. Ever since the 1801 Concordat between **Napoléon Bonaparte** and the Pope, the French State had financed the Catholic Church extensively, paying the salary of clergy, in return for some say in the nomination of Church leaders such as bishops. This was a big financial stake, especially when taken in conjunction with the Church's property holdings. The Radicals felt that more moderate Republicans were slow to move on such issues. In order to prod their colleagues into taking them into government, they were quite ready to vote with the Right and bring down moderate cabinets.

By the early 1890s a further element had entered the political scene in the shape of Socialism. The Socialists' major preoccupations were class-based;

they thought in terms of freeing workers from the oppression of capitalism and used an openly revolutionary discourse. They were scornful of national loyalties, believing that class, not nation, was what shaped people's lives. But they also shared, more perhaps than many of them realized, many essential Republican values, such as belief in parliamentary democracy and anti-Catholicism. The potential for an alliance between Socialists and Radicals, in pursuit of redistributive social and economic policies, worried mainstream Republicans.

None of the above should suggest that all French voters now accepted the Republic. Throughout the early years of the Third Republic, the Catholic Church in particular encouraged its faithful – still a numerical majority in France, though practising Catholics were probably not more than 30 per cent of the population – to vote for anti-Republican candidates. Some Catholic leaders also encouraged the anti-democratic leanings of populist figures such as General **Boulanger**, who briefly threatened to make a breakthrough on an anti-parliamentary basis in the 1880s. By the early 1890s, however, it seemed clear to Church leaders that the French Republic was probably there to stay and that Catholics needed to be better organized if they were to protect their interests within it. Their inability to mobilize had been very evident when the Ferry education laws of the 1880s were easily passed. From the late 1880s onwards, Pope Leo XIII used a series of encyclicals (statements setting out guidelines for Catholics) to urge Catholic involvement in social movements (unions, etc.) and in democratic politics. The Catholic Church's previous support for non-democratic alternatives was withdrawn.

The consequences of this realignment were soon felt. Moderate Catholics began to organize rapidly, and enough Catholic politicians were elected to form a coherent bloc and to collaborate with moderate Republican governments. Most Catholic deputies were social and economic moderates, attached to a liberal market economy and its concomitant social hierarchies. So were mainstream Republicans. They had been held apart in the past due to their opposing philosophies (rationalism versus faith), which tended to be expressed in terms of the regime: for or against the Republic. Once the regime question was out of the way, however, it became quite feasible for secularists and Catholic moderates to collaborate on practical policy issues in their shared class interest. This collaboration between different persuasions of the bourgeoisie was proceeding steadily when the Dreyfus case erupted, and it was probably the great casualty of the *affaire*.

THE *AFFAIRE* AND THE POLARIZATION OF POLITICS

As the *affaire* progressed, its initial stake (freeing a wrongly convicted individual) became subsumed in a wider struggle over Republican democracy, and, beyond this, over French identity. Within the political class and, to some extent, within France as a whole (though one should be careful of assuming that all French households followed the case every evening with passion), opinions became polarized. Broadly speaking, those on the Right tended to assume that Dreyfus had to be guilty, somewhat naïvely following the reasoning that law courts and the State which they embody do not make mistakes, and that army high commands do not make mistakes either. Others on the Right were more aware of the flimsy nature of the convicting evidence against Dreyfus. But they followed the more sinister argument that, even if some doubt remained about the reality of Dreyfus' guilt, there was no choice: Dreyfus had to remain guilty, because confidence in the authority of state institutions and the order of society would be shaken otherwise.

There was often also an overtly nationalist and/or racist element to such arguments, for Dreyfus was Jewish. The *affaire* was a period where nationalist and anti-Semitic political ideologies began to take root in the political mainstream. In the wake of defeat in the Franco-Prussian war, France's politicians and pundits had encouraged national hatred of 'the enemy without' – Germany in particular, but also other competitor countries. This quickly developed into suspicion of 'the enemy within', elements within society seen to be sapping national strength. These elements were identified variously as Communists, Socialists, anarchists, and foreigners of all sorts. Anti-Semitism gained particular strength from this widespread hostility to diversity in French society. Many commentators – and not only those on the Right – viewed Dreyfus as an undesirable, as not really French. For these anti-Semites, Dreyfus might or might not be guilty as accused, but he was certainly 'guilty' of being a Jew. In this warped view, he therefore somehow deserved to be drummed out of the army and banished. The first extract at the end of this chapter gives an example of the extent to which nationalist ideology underpinned belief in Dreyfus' guilt across the political spectrum. **Georges Clemenceau** in 1894 was ready to believe that Dreyfus was guilty. For Clemenceau at this stage the crime of betraying France to Germany was so heinous that it made the perpetrator more contemptible than the lowest beast. It should be pointed out that Clemenceau changed his opinion radically in the course of the *affaire*, and was a major supporter of Dreyfus by the late 1890s.

On the Left, people saw the implications of the case very differently. The failure to acquit Dreyfus meant that parts of the state apparatus – the judiciary, the army and those politicians who colluded with them – had got away with serious wrongdoing. If these forces were not checked, who knew how far such behaviour might go? There seemed a danger that democracy would be threatened and unrepresentative minorities seize power, overthrowing the work of the preceding two decades. The second extract at the end of this chapter, from Émile Zola's celebrated polemical letter, 'J'Accuse', demonstrates just how strongly this threat was felt. Zola decries in particular the role of the anti-Semitic press in whipping up fury against Dreyfus, and he shines light on the undemocratic forces working against justice and truth in the Dreyfus affair.

For the Left, the way to stop these undemocratic forces gaining ground was to ensure a strong Republican government, which would do justice to Dreyfus and, beyond that, would purge the remaining elements of the State that were clearly still anti-Republican. Thus was born the movement towards the 'Government of Republican Defence', which took office under **René Waldeck Rousseau** following a very polarized election campaign in 1898, where the two camps of pro- and anti-Dreyfus activists were clearly visible. On both sides, the political running was being made by the more extreme elements. The space for compromise and accommodation was suddenly closed. There was no centre any longer, and politicians and voters were forced to either Left or Right. In terms of political groups, the moderate Republicans were affected particularly cruelly, splitting into camps for or against Dreyfus. Some of them supported the campaign to revise the court verdict. It was clear to them that the Republic was threatened, and they were ready to join with Radicals and others to save it. But others took the opposing view. For them, the 'Dreyfusard' campaign struck at the heart of the French State and should be resisted. This group would oppose Waldeck Rousseau's so-called 'Government of Republican Defence', and this fundamental split in the Republican family would last for the rest of the Third Republic, right up until 1940.

In general, moderates who were pro-Dreyfus formed the core of most cabinets. The others were pushed further to the political Right, forming an umbrella party called the *Fédération Républicaine* (Republican Federation or FR). Their Republican colleagues regarded them as too suspiciously close to the Catholic Right for comfort. In time, however, they were allowed into government in small numbers. The politics of Republican Defence were simple. A government was formed including mainstream Republicans, Radicals and, for the first time, a Socialist. This government moved swiftly against the perceived alliance of authoritarians and clericals. The upper reaches of the army and judiciary were purged and a 1901 law on associations obliged religious orders to seek legal registration. This re-establishing of authority proved popular in the country, and the 1902 elections threw up a more left-leaning majority. Government passed to the Radicals, who applied the registration laws with relish, deepening the antagonism between Church and State and clearing the way for the separation of the two, which came at the end of 1905.

The anti-Republicans responded in kind. New forms of political protest emerged, with street demonstrations prominent, unsurprisingly perhaps, given that the Republicans remained in firm control of parliament. Mass movements or 'leagues' were formed, most of them stridently nationalistic. Their major preoccupation was a notion of French identity which relied heavily on excluding supposedly 'un-French' elements from society. The *Ligue Anti-Sémite* (Anti-Semitic League), for instance, made it clear even in its title that it did not regard Jews as being authentically French. Some of its inspiration came from the writings of journalist **Édouard Drumont**, whose influential book *La*

France Juive (Jewish France) mixed anti-Semitism with anti-capitalism, seeing France and French workers as being exploited by Jewish, therefore foreign and 'un-French', capitalists. Another right-wing nationalist theorizing of French identity came from **Charles Maurras**, founder of the principal of the leagues, *Action Française* (French Action or AF). The AF advocated authoritarian monarchy to remedy to what it saw as the decay of French society caused by Republicanism and its misguided notions of equality, liberty and fraternity. AF stood for a version of France that was a pre-modern, deferential, mainly rural entity, fast disappearing even as Maurras wrote about it. But that tended to be concealed by his bitter, inflammatory rhetoric, which was particularly directed against the four enemies of Frenchness: the Jew, the Freemason, the Protestant and the *métèque*, a word difficult to translate but which connotes foreignness in a very pejorative way. The direct political influence of AF would always be small (in the time-honoured manner of extremist organizations it put most of its effort into streetfighting rather than electoral politics), but its cultural impact was considerable. Many elites from conservative backgrounds were influenced by its angry, defensive notion of Frenchness and its readiness to embrace undemocratic means to root out those it identified as 'un-French'. One of the main effects of the *affaire* was to help crystallize this new, virulent preoccupation with national identity.

So during these years political extremism was a dominant force. Moderate Catholic groups failed to make a decisive breakthrough in parliament and were unable to do much to reverse the tide of anti-clerical measures. When, from 1906 onwards, French state officials began to make inventories of Church property so as to arrange for their disposal under the Separation Law, there was widespread civil resistance, some of it violent, especially in very Catholic regions like Brittany. France remained quite polarized still, and it took the efforts of more conciliatory governments to strike deals with the Church hierarchy about the disposal of Church assets and gradually to lower the temperature. By then of course, Dreyfus had long been pardoned, and the *affaire* in the strict sense was over. Yet the political passions it engendered lived on beyond it. It is now time to summarize just what this traumatic period meant for France in terms of defining its identity or, more realistically, its identities.

THE FRENCH, THEIR REPUBLIC AND THEIR IDENTITIES

Church and State

The *affaire* decanted a number of preoccupations about identity that had been there for some time. Among Republicans, it was now clear that to be a Republican embodied acceptance of what commentators have called 'the absolute Republic'. By this, they mean that for a true Republican it was never enough merely to endorse the Republican form of electoral politics and parliamentary government. By the 1890s these conditions were quite acceptable to many, especially Catholics who had previously been wary of the Republic. Moderate, progressive Republicans who were ready to work with moderate Catholics did not expect anything more from them than this minimal commitment to democracy. But 'real Republicans' expected a deeper attachment to the whole philosophical basis that underpinned Republicanism, that is to say belief in the primacy of science and reason, hence hostility to revealed religion. Beneath the apparently neutral tone of secular ideology (according to which religious beliefs are a private matter), real Republicans could only, logically, be against religion. Their attempts to distinguish between anti-clericalism and hostility to religion *per se* always had a hollow ring, for they felt a fundamental incompatibility with non-secular world-views. The minimum they could be content with was total removal of the Church from the public sphere, while they waited for the day when religious sentiment would wither away thanks to the universal spread of rationalism via state education in schools.

This world-view was an unconditional and triumphalist one, and it meant that Republicans could never really see Catholics as full partners in French political society. They would always bear a mark of Cain, as it were. Thus, for years, FR politicians would be regarded by 'real Republicans' as potential traitors, because they were believed to be willing to cut a deal with Catholics and go back on the secularist laws already enacted. That is why they never got more than the bare minimum of posts in government. The Separation Law, seen in this light, was more than just an administrative and financial measure. It was a highly symbolic act, laying claim to an exclusive definition of what was politically acceptable, and ultimately, of what was French. The *affaire* did not create any of this, it simply brought out into the open sentiments that were already there. This emotional type of Republicanism continues to enjoy a long lease of life in France. In the hands of capable politicians, its slogans and buzzwords can still mobilize large swathes of the population, especially when allied to the notions of equality and social mobility that are also part of the Republican package.

Socialism and Republicanism

One other French group also redefined its identity during this period. Before the *affaire*, Socialists had been uncertain about the Republic. They admired 1789 and the 'Declaration of the Rights of Man', but criticized formal Republican democracy for legitimizing, and indeed concealing, the power of bourgeois property owners over the rights of propertyless workers. The tendency was initially quite indifferent to the fate of Dreyfus or indeed of the democratic Republic; what mattered was class struggle between workers and bourgeois. The *affaire* changed all this. Leadership of the Socialists passed to **Jean Jaurès**, from a classic Republican background. A charismatic and skilled politician, Jaurès argued that Socialism had everything to gain from democracy. By allying with progressive bourgeois elements (like the Radicals) and gradually accumulating reforms (economic, social or cultural), the Socialists could set in train an irreversible process that would gradually lead to Socialism.

This justified support for Dreyfus, but it also involved more. Socialism increasingly took on much of the value system of 'absolute Republicanism' described above. Rubbing shoulders in government and in the lobbies with mainstream Republicans, French Socialists absorbed the Republican mindset, anti-clericalism and all. Socialists were to be found in Masonic lodges in growing numbers. In the future, this once revolutionary party would become one of the bedrocks of the system it had set out to challenge. Such behavioural tendencies were probably under way before Dreyfus, but the *affaire* gave them a powerful boost. It was a key stage on the journey of French Socialists from internationalist class-warriors to good Republican Frenchmen.

Catholic party politics

If the *affaire* sharpened Republicans' conception of their identity and led them to impose boundaries, it also affected their opponents. Catholics in particular faced a difficult choice. Moderate Catholics attempted to organize themselves politically in democratic parties such as the *Alliance Libérale Populaire* (Popular Liberal Alliance or ALP), but the electoral system made it hard for them to achieve a firm breakthrough. Catholic elites continued to invest in democratic politics, however, and to build up mass organizations in civil society. This was the case after 1918 with *Action Catholique* (Catholic Action), an umbrella grouping which included organizations for workers, women, students and farmers. This period also saw the beginnings of what would nowadays be called a Christian-Democratic party, in the shape of the *Parti Démocratique Populaire* (Popular Democratic Party or PDP). But much of this activity was on the margins of the Republic, and Catholic politicians were only very grudgingly tolerated by mainstream Republicans who continued to see French identity in secular terms. It took the defeat of 1940 and the Nazi occupation for a Catholic Resistance movement to emerge, and this played an important part in the Resistance movement. After 1945 a genuine Christian-Democratic party, the MRP, would emerge from the Resistance and play a decisive role in the post-war reconstruction of France. As explained, the closer ties between moderate Republicans and democratic Catholics were well established by the mid-1890s. But then came the *affaire*, which enabled adversaries on both sides to polarize politics again. This exclusion of moderate Catholics from mainstream political life for four decades is probably one of the least visible but most profound effects of the *affaire*.

Nationalism

Perceptions were clarified also for other adversaries of the Republic, not all of them Catholics. The *affaire* led in conservative circles generally to much questioning about what France stood for. The Dreyfus years saw the emergence of recognizable forms of modern nationalist doctrine, but now anchored firmly on the Right. For most of the nineteenth century, patriotism (only now did the word nationalism become widely used) had been identified with the Left and the whole Revolutionary tradition. The 1789 Revolution was seen as having produced a model for the modern nation–state which brought together the inhabitants of France on the basis of a shared citizenship, involving common rights and duties, rather than simply on the basis of their being born on the same territory and sharing a language or common culture.

The Revolutionary notion of nationhood was rationalistic, rather than sentimental; it was civic, rather than based on kinship ties. This conception of nationhood was predicated heavily on the white male living in mainland France, at a time when women were making their presence increasingly felt, and when France was acquiring a huge overseas empire in Africa and Asia. But these were dimensions of the debate whose importance was largely unperceived. So it was Republicanism which had championed the civic version of nationhood. In the 1890s, however, conservative theorists went back to a more ethnic, less civic version of national identity. Writers, such as Charles Maurras and **Maurice Barrès**, produced a revamped conservative version of the development of modern France. Their views were broadly the following: French society was similar to a natural organism which grew according to its own, unfathomable, logic. Attempts to hasten such growth by political or social engineering such as Republican politics would prove destructive in the end. Society was a natural, ordered, hierarchy, in which one had to know one's place and where traditional authorities like the upper class and the Church were vital ingredients of stability.

Barrès codified this pseudo-scientific conservatism in his novel *Les Déracinés* (1897), which tells of two provincial youths who do well in the Republican state education system and who come to Paris to make their fortune. The sophistication of urban life proves too much for them, however, and they fall into crime and ultimately commit murder. With them to the guillotine goes the Republican dream of education and social mobility. Barrès promotes the idea that peasants are destined to remain peasants, and that education and Republican ideology only serve to confuse people about their natural station in life. As well as being a hierarchical, organic society, France was, for Barrès, deeply traditional. For him, the French had strong emotional links to their territory, epitomized in his phrase 'la terre et les morts' (land and the dead), which tied French identity to a quasi-mythical imagining of the French past.

This brand of mystical nationalism was to have a long life. Its emphasis on attachment to land was in part a response to the losses of Alsace and Lorraine in the Franco-Prussian war of 1870 to 1871. It thus echoed loudly in the call to arms of the First World War, when France went to war partly in a spirit of *revanchisme* (seeking revenge) to regain these territories, whose loss had long been presented as a kind of physical amputation of France. Moreover, the rhetoric of 'land and the dead' continued to influence nationalism in the inter-war years, a period when economic and political difficulties again focused French minds on eradicating the 'enemy within'. Extreme right-wing polemicists such as Maurras did much to encourage a French mindset favourable to collaboration with the Nazis in the Second World War, and the notion pedalled by anti-Semites in the 1890s – that Dreyfus should be drummed out of France and the army because he was 'guilty' of being a Jew – can be seen to foreshadow the growing anti-Semitism of the 1930s and French complicity in the deportation of French Jews to the Nazi death camps during the Second World War.

CONCLUSION

Ultimately, right-wing intellectuals used the Dreyfus case to forge their own version of French identity. Anti-rational, traditionalist, conservative and hierarchical, their vision was the complete antithesis of the Republican vision of a France based on reason and science, offering gradual social, cultural and economic progress. A very real sense of 'two Frances' was forged, and these patterns would persist long into the twentieth century. The Dreyfus affair can thus be seen as a pivotal moment in the process whereby the French defined themselves in relation to each other and to their political system.

Extract 4.1: Georges Clemenceau reacts to the 'guilty' verdict on Dreyfus. Clemenceau was at first convinced of Dreyfus' guilt, as shown here, but later became one of Dreyfus' major supporters

A l'unanimité, le conseil de guerre a déclaré le capitaine Alfred Dreyfus coupable de trahison. Le crime est si épouvantable qu'on a voulu douter jusqu'au dernier moment. Un homme élevé dans la religion du drapeau, un soldat honoré de la garde des secrets de la défense nationale, trahir – mot effroyable ! – livrer à l'étranger tout ce qui peut l'aider dans les préparatifs d'une invasion nouvelle, cela paraissait impossible. Comment se trouve-t-il un homme pour un tel acte ? Comment un être humain peut-il se faire si déshonoré qu'il ne puisse attendre qu'un crachat de dégoût de ceux-là mêmes qu'il a servis ? . . .

A l'unanimité de ses juges, Alfred Dreyfus a été condamné au maximum de la peine ... Le juge a dit : la mort. Sans l'article 5 de la Constitution de 1848 qui abolit la peine de mort en matière politique, Dreyfus serait fusillé demain. . . . On ne fera jamais comprendre au public qu'on ait fusillé, il y a quelques semaines, un malheureux enfant de vingt ans coupable d'avoir jeté un bouton de sa tunique à la tête du président du conseil de guerre, tandis que le traître Dreyfus, bientôt partira pour l'île Nou, où l'attend le jardin de Candide. . . . Pour l'homme qui facilite à l'ennemi l'envahissement de la patrie, qui appelle les Bavarois de Bazeilles à de nouveaux massacres, qui ouvre le chemin aux incendiaires, aux fusilleurs, aux voleurs de territoire, aux bourreaux de la patrie une vie paisible, toute aux joies de la culture du cocotier. Il n'y a rien de si révoltant. . . .

Source: Georges Clemenceau, 1899: 'Le traître', 25 December 1894, in *L'iniquité*. Paris: Stock, pp. 2–3

The military court has unanimously declared Captain Alfred Dreyfus guilty of treason. The crime is so appalling that people wanted to doubt it up to the last moment. A man brought up to love his country's colours, a soldier honoured with keeping secrets of national defence, committing treason – what a horrifying word! – handing over to the enemy anything which might help him prepare to invade anew, it seemed impossible. How can there be a man who would commit such an act? How can a human being make himself so dishonourable that he can expect no more than to be spat on disgustedly by those very people he served? . . .

In the unanimous verdict of his judges, Alfred Dreyfus has been given the maximum sentence. . . . The judge said: death. Were it not for Article 5 of the 1848 Constitution, which abolishes the death penalty for political matters, Dreyfus would be shot tomorrow. . . . It will be impossible to make the public understand that a wretched 20-year-old boy was shot, a few weeks ago, for having thrown a button from his tunic at the president of the military court, while the traitor Dreyfus will soon depart for Nou Island, where Candide's garden awaits him. . . . For the man who helps the enemy invade the fatherland, who encourages the Bazeilles Bavarians in new slaughtering, who opens the way for arsonists, executioners, land thieves, torturers of the fatherland, a peaceful life, spent enjoying growing coconut-palms. There is nothing so scandalous.

Extract 4.2: Émile Zola denounces the miscarriage of justice in 1898

L'affaire Dreyfus était l'affaire des bureaux de la guerre, un officier de l'état-major, dénoncé par ses camarades de l'état-major, condamné sous la pression des chefs de l'état-major. Encore une fois, il ne peut revenir innocent sans que tout l'état-major soit coupable. . . . Quel coup de balai le gouvernement républicain devrait donner dans cette jésuitière . . . ! Où est-il, le ministère vraiment fort et d'un patriotisme sage qui osera tout y refondre et tout y renouveler ? Que de gens je connais qui, devant une guerre possible, tremblent d'angoisse, en sachant dans quelles mains est la défense nationale ! Et quel nid de basses intrigues, de commérages et de dilapidations, est devenu cet asile sacré, où se décide le sort de la patrie ! On s'épouvante devant le jour terrible que vient d'y jeter l'affaire Dreyfus, ce sacrifice humain d'un malheureux, d'un « sale juif » ! . . .

. . . C'est un crime de s'être appuyé sur la presse immonde ... C'est un crime . . . d'exaspérer les passions de réaction et d'intolérance, en s'abritant derrière l'odieux antisémitisme, dont la grande France libérale des droits de l'homme mourra, si elle n'en est pas guérie. C'est un crime d'exploiter le patriotisme pour des œuvres de haine, et c'est un crime, enfin, que de faire du sabre le dieu moderne, lorsque toute la science humaine est au travail pour l'œuvre prochaine de vérité et de justice.

Source: Émile Zola, 'J'accuse', *L'Aurore*, 13 January 1898.
http://abu.cnam.fr/cgi-bin/donner_html?jaccuse3, pp. 6–7

The Dreyfus affair was the affair of the war offices: a staff officer, denounced by his comrades on the General Staff, and condemned under pressure from the Chiefs of Staff. To restate it, he cannot return innocent unless the whole General Staff is guilty. . . . The government should have a good sweep out of this den of Jesuits . . .! Where is he, the minister with true strength and wise patriotism, who will dare to recast and renew everything in the General Staff? How many people do I know who, faced with possible war, tremble with anxiety, knowing the hands in which national defence lies! And what a nest of lowly intrigues, of gossiping and squandering, this sacred refuge where the country's fate is decided has turned into! The terrible light that the Dreyfus affair, this human sacrifice of a poor wretch, of a 'dirty Jew', has shone on it fills us with horror! . . .

. . . It is criminal to have relied on support from the vile press . . . It is criminal to have whipped up passion for reaction and intolerance, while hiding behind hateful anti-Semitism, from which the great, liberal France of the rights of man will die, if she is not cured of it. It is criminal to have exploited patriotism for works of hatred, and it is criminal, finally, to have turned the sword into the modern god, when the whole of human knowledge is working towards the advent of truth and justice.

FURTHER READING

Cahm, E. 1996. *The Dreyfus affair in French society and politics*. London: Longman.
    Narrative and exploration of the affair and its repercussions in France, using documentary sources. Detailed bibliographies.
Hanley, D. 2002. *Party, government, society: Republican democracy in France*. Oxford: Berghahn.
    A more theoretical explanation of the importance of parties in French Republican politics.
Mayeur, J.-M. 1984. *La vie politique sous la Troisième République*. Paris: Seuil.
Réberioux, M. 1975. *La République radicale? 1898–1914*. Paris: Seuil.
    Still two of the clearest guides to the background politics of the period, both by renowned historians.
Rudelle, O. and Berstein, S. 1992. *Le modèle républicain*. Paris: Presses Universitaires de Paris.
    Clear exposition of the origins, development and promotion of the French Republican model, with special emphasis on the 'golden age of Republicanism', 1900–39.

5

The First World War, 1914–18: death of the old world, birth of a new?

Cheryl Koos

INTRODUCTION

This chapter will examine the searing impact of the First World War – what was then called the Great War – on the formation of French Republican identity. In the years preceding the war, French society and politics were engulfed by the twin processes of industrialization and modernization. The fledgling Third Republic and its leaders confronted increasing demands for political inclusion in the Republican ideal emanating from working-class men and women, as well as middle-class women. French society wrestled with the question: to whom did liberty, equality and fraternity apply? With the French declaration of war and the subsequent German invasion of France in 1914, the Republic called upon its citizens to set aside these battles in order to unite behind a common cause – a *union sacrée* (sacred union) – that would defeat the Germans and preserve France. The *union sacrée* initially succeeded in persuading feuding political parties and groups to set aside their differences in a common defence of the Republic. However, the social, cultural and political tensions that accompanied the devastating conflict would shape and influence the post-war era, laying the seeds of discontent that would result in the Third Republic's collapse in 1940.

THE REPUBLIC ON THE EVE OF WAR

In turn-of-the-century France, debates about national strength centred on the declining birthrate and the need to industrialize. Political and cultural leaders saw increased numbers of children and production of manufactured goods as vital to the Republic's survival in a world dominated by the British Empire and German military ambition. But the government's efforts to increase the birthrate and spur industrial production met powerful challenges. Republican fears about declining birthrates clashed with changing gender roles. In the late nineteenth century, women increasingly laid claim to the Republican ideals of liberty and equality. A vocal women's movement advocated political and social rights, such as the vote and women's access to higher education. This resulted in more women postponing marriage and motherhood at a time when the nation called them to re-engage in their traditional roles.

At the same time, a growing trade union movement campaigned for worker's rights, and labour laws challenged the Republic from the left of the political spectrum. Having withstood the challenge from the nationalist Right in the wake of the **Dreyfus** affair of the 1890s, the Republic's leaders clamped down on dissent. In spite of this, the trade union movement, led by Socialists such as **Jean Jaurès**, attracted support and forced the government to negotiate with the workforce as a wave of massive strikes crippled industry.

Amid rising domestic crises (and perhaps as a result of them), French political leaders attempted to increase France's power globally by expanding the French empire. Conflicts over imperial gains in Africa brought tensions between France and Germany to breaking point in the early years of the new century. Encouraged by notions of racial superiority that pitted one nation against another, international pressure increased dramatically. Soon, France had formed the Triple Entente with Russia and Great Britain opposing the Triple Alliance, comprised of Germany, Austria-Hungary and the Ottoman Empire. Even regarding foreign policy, however, the Third Republic faced vocal critics. A powerful internationalist worker's movement, avowedly pacifist, condemned imperialist projects and yet also called for *revanche* (revenge) against Germany.

OUTBREAK OF WAR

On 28 June 1914, the Austrian Archduke Francis Ferdinand was assassinated in Sarajevo. This set in motion a series of events that resulted in war. Domestically, a quickly emerging nationalist consensus drowned out the anti-war French Left and all opposition to the war essentially ended when the Socialist legislator Jean Jaurès was murdered in a Parisian café in July the same year. Germany intended to eliminate the Western Front first, by sweeping through Belgium to Paris, then turning to Russia in the east. With this war strategy in mind, Germany declared war on 3 August 1914 and promptly invaded Belgium. German troops entered France within several weeks and, by 3 September 1914, the German army was within 50 km (30 miles) of Paris. Formerly bitter enemies within French society and politics closed ranks in defence of the Republic. This common cause – the *union sacrée* (sacred union) – united the nation in order to preserve the Republic and its ideals in the face of German barbarism and militarism.

The German army's initial advance took the French nation by surprise. Only an eleventh-hour stand, the Battle of the Marne, stopped the German army 21 km (13 miles) from Paris and forced them to retreat to the Aisne River. To halt the attack, the French army mobilized every available Parisian taxicab to pour French troops into battle. As a result, the German advance was bogged down and Paris was saved for the time being, but the war was far from over.

WAR ON TWO FRONTS

With the initial declaration of war in August 1914, French soldiers and military leaders anticipated a short war of perhaps just six weeks. 'To Berlin' was the clarion call that propelled the French army into its early battles. Shortly, however, what had been anticipated on both sides as a quick and decisive war degenerated into a stalemate. The line drawn following the Battle of the Marne became the unmoving front. The British and French on one side and the Germans on the other dug in for the duration. Each side created a system of trenches throughout northern and eastern France in which their soldiers lived, fought, survived and died for five long years.

The type of warfare that ensued differed completely from previous military models. Both sides had prepared for a war similar to nineteenth-century wars but new and more deadly weaponry, including long-range cannons and variations on the machine gun, changed the landscape of war. Officers threw men 'over the top' of trenches into a hail of artillery fire coming from machine gun nests and precise shelling, dramatically increasing casualty counts but not the amount of enemy territory taken. As a result, France was in reality two nations: the home front, in which civilians continued their daily routine, and this separate world of the trenches, one in which men lived and died in sub-human and unspeakable conditions.

Life in the trenches

In many respects, the world of the trenches provoked one of the arguably fullest manifestations of the Republican ideals of equality and fraternity. The horrific conditions of everyday trench life brought together men from all walks of French life. Neither the officer of significant means and education nor the lowliest *poilu* (front-line soldier) were able to escape incessant shelling, gas attacks and rotting and dismembered bodies. The rats, the lice, the mud, the inclement weather, and the threat of impending death did not discriminate according to class, status or wealth. The combatants' shared experience created a bond that soldiers and historians alike would later idealize as the 'fraternity of the trenches'. Many veterans would remember the camaraderie at the front with fondness and would later yearn for the 'spirit of the trenches' to be reawakened in post-war political movements and veterans' groups. One could say that the realization of these Republican values would provide the seeds of discontent that would ultimately challenge the legitimacy of the Republic itself and contribute to its demise; for some of those who experienced such extreme situations sought to reproduce them in civilian life when the war was over.

The battle at Verdun, a fortress in north-eastern France, in 1916 became one of the most tragic and gruesome events in trench warfare's bloody history. By attacking this historic fort system, the Germans assumed correctly that the French military would throw all of its energies into defending the position. On 21 February 1916, the Germans attacked French positions and continued to do so around the clock for the next ten months. Led by General **Henri-Philippe Pétain**, the French army dug in and fired back. Essentially, the French high command and the government saw this as the 'make-or-break' battle of the war. Pétain poured all available men and material into Verdun's defence. Conditions were so devastating and demoralizing for the French soldiers that Pétain rotated each French regiment through Verdun hoping to shorten the horror individual soldiers experienced. Every army regiment spent eight days in this hell of continuous shelling; on average, half of each regiment died. One regiment arrived with 1,200 soldiers; by day eight, only 98 had survived. While Pétain's strategy worked and the battle eventually ended in December, over 163,000 French soldiers were dead along with 143,000 Germans, and several hundred thousand were wounded on each side. Other battles, such as those at the Marne and Somme, would also be the sites of terrible loss of life and human tragedy but in the French collective memory, even today, Verdun represents both the bravery and futility of trench warfare during the First World War.

The Home Front

On leave, soldiers encountered a world very different to that of the trenches. The gulf between the front and the rear was exacerbated by the fact that civilians understood little of the soldiers' experiences due to propagandist news reports and government censorship. Upon leaving the trenches, the *poilus* entered a world in which people went about their daily routines seemingly unaffected by the nightmarish conditions only scores of kilometres away. It was a world largely inhabited by women who, like their counterparts in Great Britain and Germany, were 'doing their bit' for national defence in order to secure the future of the Republic.

Women filled numerous roles in the wartime economy. As the war continued and mobilization increased, so did the need for women to fill the roles vacated by men forced to go to the front lines. In a stark example of the male workforce exodus, the percentage of the mobilized male workforce increased from 30 per cent in 1914 to 63 per cent in 1918. Peasant women worked tirelessly to save their family farms, while urban working-class women who worked in traditionally female occupations, such as the garment industry, moved to more economically lucrative, though dangerous, positions in heavy industry. Such opportunities mushroomed after 1916 with demands for a greater munitions output as a result of the defence of Verdun. These *munitionettes* became celebrated figures, fêted by politicians and journalists for their vital role in the war effort. Women also replaced men as bus and tram drivers, fare collectors, post office and bank clerks, and even as café servers.

While women who did their patriotic duty were praised at the outset of the war for their efforts, they were soon criticized for their actions. Politicians, labour leaders and cultural commentators were initially sympathetic to working women who were forced into new situations because of wartime needs and their own economic circumstances. However, as the war continued, these same figures grew to view women's participation in the war economy with a combination of blame and suspicion. These former heroines were turned into villains who were taking advantage of the soldiers' misery for their own personal gain. As fears about women's economic and cultural emancipation grew, politicians and conservative cultural commentators attempted to reformulate women's wartime duties. Women's utmost duty to the Republic, they agreed, lay not in taking men's jobs, but in producing more French children in order to replace the many Frenchmen lost on the battlefield. Here, pre-war pro-natalist rhetoric, which called for an increase in the birthrate, reappeared with renewed urgency. Groups, such as the National Alliance for the Increase of the French Birthrate and for Life, led calls for women to return to the home and focus on the family, particularly by giving birth to France's future. With a growing pro-natalist consensus, government censors sought to muzzle vocal pre-war birth control advocates who, in conjunction with pacifists, urged women to resist these calls.

Fears about women's economic emancipation as valued workers became realized in women's changing appearance. Corsets and tight-fitting, ankle-length dresses became a thing of the past while short, bobbed hair and waistless dresses grew in popularity. This androgynous look caused conservatives to wring their hands over the changes that the war had wrought. As soldier and later fascist novelist **Pierre Drieu la Rochelle** would lament, France was becoming a 'civilization that no longer had sexes'. Similarly, front-line soldiers worried about the ramifications of women's increased wartime independence on the shape of post-war society.

THREATS TO THE REPUBLIC AND THE WAR EFFORT

The brutality and duration of trench warfare gradually created cracks in the nation's wartime unity. From the war's outset, the social divisions that were growing prior to 1914 slowly bubbled to the surface of political life again.

With the initial German advance of August and September 1914, disparate political foes had set aside their differences to rally around the flag and the French war effort. This show of unity succeeded in marginalizing and driving underground any opposition. Not all political unity was voluntary, though.

The government imposed harsh censorship early on in the war, drastically curtailing freedom of the press and speech. However, the poor organization of the government upon the swift German attack gave way to the first internal assault on the Republic with the imposition of martial law on the country. General **Joffre**, following the Battle of the Marne in September 1914, persuaded government officials to accept a plan that would allow the military to direct the country and the war effort. With the legislative chambers inactive for four months following the temporary displacement of the government from Paris to Bordeaux, Joffre and his administrators enjoyed free rein. They imposed strict censorship on the press and on opposing viewpoints and decreed that the army could arrest civilians and other non-combatants who violated their edicts. By 1915, the elected government had reasserted itself, regaining its control over the non-military sector. It took over the direction of the economy and particularly war production after Joffre's plans at home and on the battlefield were challenged.

Even though the constitutional Republic triumphed over the military at this early stage in the war, the government was under extreme pressure as casualties mounted and the war continued with no end in sight. German forces occupied northern France, subjecting the French citizens of that region to military administration and harsh conditions. Press censorship limited public knowledge about what was occurring at the front, thus creating increased impatience among the civilians who could not understand why the *poilus*, if so victorious, could not win the war once and for all. Similarly, the front-line soldiers grew impatient with the inability of those at home to comprehend the conditions they faced. They were also resentful of a government that refused to tell the truth about the war and the casualty count.

Following the ten-month siege of Verdun, the army was at the point of exhaustion, further threatening the government's ability to continue and win the war. The new commander, General **Nivelle**, redesigned battle strategy and began plans in early 1917 for a major new offensive intended to realize the elusive 'breakthrough'. In a two-week campaign that began in April 1917, Nivelle and his commanders sent wave after wave of *poilus* 'over the top' to attack well-fortified German positions. By the end of the fortnight, nearly 150,000 men were dead. Driven by the unremitting carnage, the front-line soldiers mutinied against their officers who ordered them to attack. They simply refused to submit to almost certain death. They did not oppose fighting, but they mutinied against the senseless offensive. Fearing news of the army's disintegration would reach either Paris or Berlin, the government acted quickly, replacing Nivelle with General Pétain, the victor of Verdun. Order was quickly restored and Pétain court-martialled more than 3,000 and had 49 men executed. To prevent further disturbances, he acted to improve morale by authorizing more leave time and better food. This combination, along with the refusal to engage in wasteful offensives, worked and the army never mutinied again.

Concerns about the war also increased at home. Even though the government refused to release casualty figures, the number of widows and orphans multiplied as did the number of *mutilés*, soldiers who were permanently maimed. Graphic descriptions of trench life and battle conditions also made it through the censor's net. **Henri Barbusse**, a front-line soldier and journalist, published *Le feu* (translated in English as *Under fire*) in 1916. Selling over 230,000 copies in its first year of publication, *Le feu* chronicled for the French public what it suspected: that the war was nothing other than mass carnage that had cut down the prime of French manhood. In addition, Barbusse drew clearly the stark divide between the *poilus* and the home front (see Extract 5.1).

Civilian unrest mounted in 1917 and early 1918, as prices rose and food rationing became a reality. Labour strikes resumed in 1917 after a hiatus for the first two years of the war. Prominent political figures in the Radical and Socialist parties took steps toward a negotiated peace. Former Radical Prime Minister **Joseph Caillaux** even went so far as to meet with an Italian politician in the hope of forming a coalition that would end the fighting. Political infighting racked the government for the first time since 1914. By 1917, the *union sacrée* was a thing of the past.

In an effort to stem the mounting criticism of the war and dissension within the government, the current President of the Republic elevated **Georges Clemenceau** to Prime Minister. Known as the 'Tiger' for his political ruthlessness, Clemenceau essentially declared war against politicians like Caillaux who expressed interest in a negotiated peace. Labelling such opponents 'defeatists', Clemenceau took firm control. Dissent in any form was forbidden; the government prosecuted Caillaux for treason and, although he was eventually acquitted, he never recovered his political footing. Clemenceau threatened former Prime Minister **Aristide Briand**, another advocate of negotiation, to the extent that he bowed out of politics under the same threat. Civilian pacifists were arrested, tried and convicted for their anti-war views. While Clemenceau held the government together, he did so at the expense of the basic tenets of the Republic. A civilian dictatorship, in cooperation with the military, sacrificed 'liberty, equality, and fraternity' for the duration. After the crackdown on dissent – and some argue because of it – France weathered the final year of the war with the aid of American and British troops taking part in most attacks on the enemy.

Hélène Brion and pacifism

As anti-war sentiment increased during 1917, the government became more pro-active in its denunciation of pacifists and 'defeatists'. One woman who became a symbol for the Clemenceau government's attempts to limit dissent was **Hélène Brion**. Arrested on 18 November 1917 (the day after Clemenceau became Prime Minister), the nursery school teacher from Paris was taken into custody for passing out anti-war pamphlets. For both the political Right and Left, Brion represented what was wrong with French society and politics, though for very different reasons. For the Right, she epitomized the public woman who violated her 'natural' role as mother, instead speaking out publicly against the government. For the Left, she stood as an example both of women's powerlessness in the face of governmental persecution and of women's strength for holding to her convictions in the face of concerted efforts to demonize her.

As an active feminist and Socialist, Hélène Brion had participated in many political causes before her arrest. She was a union leader with the National Federation of Teachers and had risen quickly up their administrative ranks with the sudden vacancies left by mobilized men. At her trial, despite the efforts of the prosecutors and the right-wing press, Brion mounted an eloquent defence, bringing in notable figures who testified to her good moral character. She defended herself by asserting women's duty to save France and to preserve its future, effectively turning pro-war propaganda on its head. As a woman and a feminist, she argued, she wanted to protect and save France's children and to preserve its core values of liberty and justice. While Brion was convicted, the presiding judge sentenced her to a three-year suspended sentence, meaning she would not serve time in prison. Brion ultimately become a symbol of defiance against an increasingly authoritarian government that compromised the central Republican values of liberty, equality and fraternity. In time, it would eventually extend those notions to include sisterhood, as well as brotherhood.

VICTORY AND PEACE?

With the entry of the United States into the conflict, the Allies undertook a series of offensives and counter-offensives in the summer of 1918. When the firing finally ceased with the armistice of 11 November 1918, a victorious France was a nation irreparably changed by the four long years of war. All that had seemed solid, as one critic wrote, had melted into air. The Third Republic survived, but French society and culture bore little resemblance to that of the years preceding the hostilities. While France had won the war, would it win the peace?

Domestic consequences

The war's toll on France can be most accurately measured by the human price its citizens paid. Between 1.3 and 1.4 million French soldiers lost their lives. Essentially, this cataclysmic statistic meant that one-tenth of all adult men had been killed. In addition, over 1,300,000 surviving soldiers were severely disabled, 300,000 of whom were classified as 'maimed', those whose injuries were so incapacitating that they were not able to work. Over 600,000 women were widowed, many of whom had children. Countless other women lost fiancés or boyfriends and, because most of the war was fought on French soil, thousands of families lost their homes and livelihoods.

Central to Republican concerns for decades had been France's problematic birthrate; given the human losses of the war, such worries were catapulted to centre-stage. With so many adult men dead and the resulting imbalance in the ratio between women and men, politicians and social commentators fixated on the need to produce large numbers of children quickly, presumably to fight in the next war with Germany and to staff its factories. The *jeune femme moderne*, the young modern woman who had emerged from the war with increased social and economic independence, quickly became the target of these worries. Social conservatives urged women to perform their duty and give birth to the children that the nation so desperately needed. These appeals clashed with feminist arguments that patriotic French women who had so diligently served their country for four traumatic years deserved the vote, finally making them full partners in the Republican ideal. Such aspirations were dashed by a combination of conservative anxieties about women's changing social roles and radical concerns that giving women the vote would destroy the Republic. Leftist politicians perceived women to be in thrall to their priests and more likely to vote for right-wing or monarchist candidates. A draft bill proposing women's suffrage was defeated in the Upper Chamber, known as the Senate, in 1922.

In addition to the many war memorials erected to honour the dead, living memorials to the atrocity of war haunted the streets of French cities, towns and villages. Men who had survived the war shocked those left at home with their missing limbs, disfigured faces and psychological scars. Upon their return, such men encountered a world that had turned upside down. Many were unable to reassert their roles as family breadwinners because of their physical or psychological wounds and they were forced to yield their traditional roles to their wives and children. To cope with the challenges of living in such a changed environment, many veterans turned to newly formed veterans' groups composed of survivors of the trenches who desired the steadfast camaraderie that had enabled them to endure the hellish conditions. While some veterans' groups dedicated themselves to pacifist causes, others were intensely nationalistic and contributed to a rightward trend in French politics immediately following the war. The first post-war legislative elections ushered in what came to be called the 'Blue Horizon Chamber', so called because of the large number of veterans who were elected. Also called the *Bloc National*, this government was the most conservative and nationalistic since the founding of the Third Republic.

International consequences

The Great War's international ramifications had a profound impact on how France conceived of itself as a nation. The Treaty of Versailles brought the four-year war to an official close with France emerging as the victor. It regained the provinces of Alsace and Lorraine which had been lost to Germany, thus re-expanding its territorial borders and reincorporating many German-speaking French citizens into the nation's fold. France also added to its empire by appropriating German territory in Africa, territory that had been French until the pre-First World War colonial skirmishes in Morocco. Clemenceau pushed for reparations from Germany, arguing that they would help rebuild French industry damaged by the occupation of northern France and the destruction of coal mines in those regions. In spite of less hard-line attitudes from the French Left and US President Woodrow Wilson, Clemenceau prevailed on many points, including reparations and the occupation of the Ruhr Valley to ensure the transfer of coal to France.

The punitive peace settlement was perceived by many to increase the chances of German aggression at a later date. Efforts were made, therefore, to ameliorate the harshness of the Versailles settlement. Aristide Briand attempted to use the weight of the newly created League of Nations to forge reconciliation with the Germans. The resulting Locarno Pact of 1925 was heralded throughout France and the world as a step toward a definitive peace, one that had not seemed assured with the war's conclusion. The pact with Germany guaranteed the two countries' mutual borders. France's efforts in the 1920s to promote peace in its foreign policy underscored a strong current of pacifism in a country whose land and people had been physically and emotionally scarred by the Great War.

CONCLUSION: REPERCUSSIONS INTO THE INTER-WAR PERIOD

1924 was a year that set the stage for political battles between the Right and the Left that would culminate in 1940 with the defeat of Republican France and the creation of the Vichy regime. The conservative *Bloc National* provoked a reaction among the Republican Left soon after it came to power by giving the Catholic Church more power than it had enjoyed since the early

Third Republic. It reacted strongly against social reforms from the war period, passing restrictive measures against birth control and abortion. It also failed to offer solutions to rising inflation. In reaction to the *Bloc*'s policies, a left-leaning coalition, the *Cartel des Gauches*, soundly defeated nationalist conservatives in elections in 1924.

The conservative reaction to the *Cartel des Gauches'* victory was swift and loud. Almost overnight, France witnessed the sudden and rapid growth of reactionary political movements that were anti-Republican, anti-parliamentary, anti-Socialist, vehemently pro-Catholic, pro-family, and pro-natalist. Not only were these groups a response to the political Left, they were also a response to the social and cultural changes wrought by the Great War. These political leagues comprised the 'first wave' of French fascism and modelled themselves on Italian fascism to a degree, but were thoroughly 'French'. Members were mostly former veterans and young idealists who were hyper-nationalistic and focused on France and the development of a 'true' French identity. Groups, like the *Jeunesses Patriotes* (Young Patriots), desired an authoritarian dictator who would remedy the decadence that they believed plagued the Republican system. While right-wing supporters disagreed as to who should be that leader, they all agreed on the qualities he must have, qualities that stemmed from the 'spirit of the trenches': honour, courage, virility, bravery and strength.

These movements were short-lived. The conditions that had characterized the rise of fascist groups in Italy and Germany did not prevail in France in the 1920s. By the 1930s, however, new opportunities presented themselves to the Far Right. The effects of the Great Depression of 1929 and a growing disaffection with the parliamentary Right and Left led to a resurgence of paramilitary, fascist activity in the early 1930s. Groups like the *Croix de Feu* (Fiery Cross), the *Solidarité Française* (French Solidarity), and the *Francistes* (Francists) all garnered greater public support than their 1920s' precursors by once again pitting their 'virile' ideologies against 'impotent parliamentarianism'. Political tensions erupted onto the streets of Paris on 6 February 1934 when mass demonstrations turned into an attempted *coup d'état*. Newly appointed Prime Minister, Radical **Édouard Daladier** resigned in the wake of the violence and was replaced with a right-wing premier who placated some on the extreme Right.

While the unrest of February 1934 did not overthrow the Republic as some had hoped, it did succeed on a major, though unintended front. It galvanized and united a fractured Left. Fears of fascism and the violence of these paramilitary groups united the Left into a 'Popular Front' made up of centre-left Radicals, Socialists and Communists. The strategy worked and the Popular Front won elections in 1936. Led by Socialist **Léon Blum**, the Popular Front government embarked on an ambitious programme of social reform to address worker grievances that had been ignored since 1914. In the face of renewed strikes during the summer of 1936, Blum and the legislature acted to institute a 40-hour working week, paid holidays for rank-and-file workers and collective bargaining agreements with unions like the powerful *Confédération Générale des Travailleurs* (General Confederation of Labour, CGT). While women's suffrage was not addressed, Blum made symbolic progress on the issue of women's rights by appointing three women to his cabinet.

The extreme Right, though, did not go away with the Popular Front's victory. After one year, the Popular Front collapsed and the politics in general drifted to the right of the political spectrum. While Blum outlawed the fascist leagues shortly after assuming office, the largest league, the *Croix de Feu*, remade itself into a parliamentary political party, the *Parti Social Français* (French Social Party, PSF). By 1938 the PSF, led by former colonel **François de la Rocque**, had more than one million members and seemed poised to make great gains in the next election. However, in 1939, war would intervene, bringing new challenges and new threats to the Republican ideals of liberty, equality and fraternity.

In conclusion, the Great War drastically changed the way in which the French thought about themselves, their political system and their place in the world. It deeply affected the structures of everyday existence and the ways in which people interpreted their lives within the larger schemes of society, politics and culture. The France of 1914 had irrevocably changed by the war's end in 1918 and, while the French Republic survived the war intact, the country struggled to find its political and economic moorings. The political battles that would follow throughout the 1920s and 1930s had their roots in the Great War. The emergence of fascism during the inter-war period was intimately connected to the violence and glorification of the trench experience. Indeed, the growing presence of fascism in French public life would ultimately threaten the Republic in new and profound ways between 1940 and 1944.

Extract 5.1: From the controversial war novel *Le feu* (1916) by Henri Barbusse

On est prêt. Les hommes se rangent, toujours en silence, avec leur couverture en sautoir, la jugulaire du casque au menton, appuyés sur leurs fusils. Je regarde leurs faces crispées, pâlies, profondes. Ce ne sont pas des soldats: ce sont des hommes. Ce ne sont pas des aventuriers, des guerriers, faits pour la boucherie humaine – bouchers ou bétail. Ce sont des laboureurs et des ouvriers qu'on reconnaît dans leurs uniformes. Ce sont des civils déracinés. Ils sont prêts. Ils attendent le signal de la mort et du meurtre; mais on voit, en contemplant leurs figures entre les rayons verticaux des baïonnettes, que ce sont simplement des hommes.

Chacun sait qu'il va apporter sa tête, sa poitrine, son ventre, son corps tout entier, tout nu, aux fusils braqués d'avance, aux obus, aux grenades accumulées et prêtes, et surtout à la méthodique et presque infaillible mitrailleuse – à tout ce qui attend et se tait effroyablement là-bas – avant de trouver les autres soldats qu'il faudra tuer. . . . On voit ce qu'il y a de songe et de peur, et d'adieu dans leur silence, leur immobilité, dans le masque de calme qui leur étreint surhumainement le visage. Ce ne sont pas le genre de héros qu'on croit, mais leur sacrifice a plus de valeur que ceux qui ne les ont pas vus ne seront jamais capables de le comprendre.

Ils attendent. L'attente s'allonge, s'éternise.

Source: Henri Barbusse, 1916: *Le feu: journal d'une escouade*. Paris: Flammarion, pp. 265–6

We are ready. The men marshal themselves, still silently, their blankets crosswise, the helmet-strap on the chin, leaning on their rifles. I look at their pale, contracted, and reflective faces. They are not soldiers, they are men. They are not adventurers, or warriors, or made for human slaughter, neither butchers nor cattle. They are labourers and artisans whom one recognizes in their uniforms. They are civilians uprooted, and they are ready. They await the signal for death or murder; but you may see, looking at their faces between the vertical gleams of their bayonets, that they are simply men.

Each one know that he is going to take his head, his chest, his belly, his whole body, and all naked, up to the rifles pointed forward, to the shells, to the bombs piled and ready, and above all to the methodical and almost infallible machine-guns – to all that is waiting for him yonder and is so frightfully silent – before he reaches the other soldiers that he must kill. . . . One sees the thought and the fear and the farewell that there is in their silence, their stillness, in the mask of tranquillity which unnaturally grips their faces. They are not the kind of hero one thinks of, but their sacrifice has greater worth than they who have not seen them will ever be able to understand.

They are waiting; a waiting that extends and seems eternal.

Source: Henri Barbusse, trans. Fitzwater Wray, 1917: *Under fire: story of a squad*. New York: E. P. Dutton, pp. 250–1

FURTHER READING

Darrow, M. 2000. *French women and the First World War*. Oxford: Berg.
Excellent overview and analysis of Frenchwomen's participation and roles during the Great War.

Popkin, J. 1994. *A history of modern France*. Englewood Cliffs, NJ: Prentice-Hall.
Includes an excellent overview of the Great War and inter-war period.

Roberts, M. L. 1994. *Civilization without sexes: reconstructing gender in France, 1917–1927*. Chicago: University of Chicago Press.
Singularly important study that examines women's gender roles in the late 1910s and 1920s.

6

The Second World War, 1939–45: divided selves

Claire Gorrara

INTRODUCTION

This chapter will examine the German Occupation of France from 1940 to 1944 as a pivotal time for French national identity. The war years represented a radical departure from life under the pre-war Third Republic and particularly the left-wing heritage of the Popular Front government (1936–37). In the wake of the shattering defeat of France by Germany in 1940, Republican democracy was replaced by the dictatorship of the Vichy regime, the wartime government of France. Vichy promoted the values of hierarchy, order and self-sacrifice and campaigned to transform French society in line with right-wing ideals. This vision was opposed by the Resistance, a loose coalition of individuals and movements who struggled for national liberation with the help of the Allied powers, Britain, America and Soviet Russia. Both Vichy and the Resistance were aware of the need to mobilize support for their cause. This chapter will explore, therefore, the values and visions that pitted Vichy against the Resistance as they appealed for the hearts and minds of the French people.

DEFEAT AND OCCUPATION

On 3 September 1939, Britain and France declared war on Germany two days after its invasion of Poland. But, until May 1940, France found itself engaged in a 'phoney war' as conscripted troops waited for German attack along the Maginot Line. This was a complex system of defences stretching across France's eastern border and included underground strong posts linked by anti-tank weapons and state-of-the-art machinery. Such a battle plan was hugely expensive and, when put to the test, proved useless in the face of German *Blitzkrieg* or 'lightning war' of combined air and land assault. French troops were defeated in just four weeks in June 1940. Nearly two million French troops were captured, the vast majority of whom would spend the next four years in prisoner-of-war camps in Germany. Eight million refugees took to the roads in northern and eastern France in an unprecedented exodus to escape the German advance.

France's defeat can be attributed to two main factors. First, France had made the strategic error of waging a defensive rather than a modern offensive war. Although the military would later argue that the German army had been better equipped and armed, this was not the case. A certain General **Charles de Gaulle**, promoted to Under-Secretary of War in May 1940, had criticized this strategic choice but had been talked down by army chiefs. Second, the defeat had its roots in the inter-war period, the years that had witnessed the advent of fascism in Germany and Italy and the bloody conflicts of the Spanish Civil War (1936–39). Although France did not experience a similar rise to power of fascist politicians, anti-parliamentary leagues and the economic depression of the early 1930s certainly shook French confidence in the Republic as an institution able to guide the nation through difficult times. However, in the aftermath of right-wing violence on the streets of Paris in February 1934, voters turned towards a newly galvanized left-wing coalition called the Popular Front and elected it to power in 1936. This short-lived administration led by **Léon Blum** revolutionized the lives of French workers, instituting paid holidays for the first time, a 40-hour working week and collective bargaining. Defeated in June 1937, the Popular Front was remembered by right-wing elements in French society as a government that had unleashed a spirit of individualism and decadence that needed to be purged from the nation. The wartime Vichy regime was, in many respects, conceived as a conscious antidote to such progressive democratic politics.

With much of France in disarray, the French government of the Third Republic left Paris for Bordeaux and then for Vichy. Faced with military defeat and the shock of invasion, parliamentarians gathered at Vichy had the choice to opt for government in exile, like a number of occupied countries, or to take the risk that French interests would be better served by collaboration with the German invader. They chose the latter course and voted to end the Third Republic in July 1940. Full powers were given to the 84-year-old Marshal **Henri-Philippe Pétain** to revise the constitution and to head a new French state named after the spa town where it had been created: Vichy. Pétain's reputation as a First World War General and hero commanded universal respect and admiration. He had remained aloof from the party politics of the Third Republic and presented himself as a candidate of unity who would rally the country. For many French people, traumatized in the aftermath of defeat, he appeared as a saviour who would deliver France from catastrophe and enable a return to normality.

Pétain and his supporters hoped to bring about national unity by imposing their vision of France, its traditions and values. Yet this project was jeopardized by the division of France into various zones under the crushing conditions of the armistice signed with Germany in June 1940. The two main zones were the occupied zone to the north, overseen by German military authorities in Paris, and the unoccupied zone, administered by the Vichy government, comprising most of southern France. This arrangement lasted until 11 November 1942 when German forces invaded the whole of France. The German decision to leave southern France under French control for part of the war was driven by practical considerations. Having the French police themselves saved German manpower for frontline battles in Soviet Russia and elsewhere. By late 1942, with the British and American military invasion of North Africa, it became imperative to stamp German domination on France in a 'total war'. Even after this time, Vichy continued to exert influence over both zones, administering domestic legislation and cooperating with the demands of the German authorities.

COLLABORATION, THE VICHY REGIME AND THE NATIONAL REVOLUTION

Collaboration with the German invader took on different forms in occupied France. There were those ideologues in Paris who admired and supported a Nazi vision of a New World Order, such as **Jacques Doriot**'s fascist *Parti Populaire Français* (French Popular Party, PPF). Others worked with and for the German authorities to further individual careers or exploited the war economy to make great profits. In terms of state collaboration, Pétain announced the intentions of the Vichy government in his symbolic handshake with Hitler at Montoire in October 1940. However, what began as a form of coexistence had transformed into a far more servile and compromised arrangement by the end of the war. Vichy collaborated in the mass deportations of Jews from France to death camps in eastern Europe and allowed the French economy and its workers to become increasingly involved in Germany's war effort.

The Vichy regime was a dictatorial form of government founded on right-wing principles. For many French people in the early days of the war, Vichy seemed to offer the hope of some protection from the worst excesses of German invasion. A common myth circulated that Pétain and Vichy were playing a 'double game', appearing to concede to German demands but safeguarding French interests. Yet the regime was more than a mere holding operation in the face of war. It represented a rejection of French Republican traditions. It was the triumph of right-wing factions who had been denied power under the Third Republic and had fiercely opposed the Popular Front government and its innovations. Such a group was not ideologically united and reactionary politicians and technocrats from many different backgrounds vied for power under the leadership of Pétain. However, the common factor linking these diverse factions was the view that French society needed to be reformed. This campaign for national renewal was christened the 'National Revolution' and became a lynchpin of Pétain's vision for a resurgent French nation.

The National Revolution was based on a visceral rejection of inter-war French democratic politics and the legacy of French Republicanism. Elected legislatures were perceived to be weak and ineffectual and much of the blame for the debacle of June 1940 was laid at the door of the Third Republic. In February 1942, the Vichy regime attempted to try Republican politicians, including Léon Blum, for France's wartime defeat but the trial was interrupted by the German authorities when it became clear that it was turning to the advantage of the accused. In contrast to its predecessor, the Third Republic, the Vichy regime promised to reinvigorate France, building on the conservative values of discipline, order, thriftiness and courage. The National Revolution was focused on supporting traditional institutions, such as the Catholic Church, and a number of organizations were created to promote the values and ideals of the National Revolution, such as *Légion des Volontaires Français Contre le Bolshevisme* (Legion of French Volunteers Against Bolshevism). This was devoted to combating another enemy of the Vichy regime, Communism. Vichy's hopes for a revitalized France were encapsulated in the motto *famille, travail, patrie* (family, work, homeland). This new motto echoed but erased the Republican motto of liberty, equality, fraternity. In choosing these ideals, Vichy set up the battle lines opposing its vision of France to that of pre-war Republican France.

Family

If the Republican motto placed great emphasis on the equality of all citizens, the Vichy regime wanted to create a social order based on 'natural' hierarchies. At the top stood Pétain as sole ruler, advised by a coterie of politicians, prominent among these **Pierre Laval**, twice Prime Minister under the Vichy regime. As the 'father of the nation', Pétain's role was to transcend social divisions and to appeal directly to the French population, a feat he achieved with considerable success in the early years of the regime. This autocratic style of government aimed to convince people that hierarchy, order and self-sacrifice were the remedy to all France's ills and would regenerate the nation.

The family played a central role in the propaganda war to win the French over to this reactionary social order. Fathers had absolute authority over wives and children and women's legal and civil rights were restricted by legislation. Divorce was made impossible in the first three years of marriage and the Vichy regime introduced draconian laws that made abortion a capital offence, punishable by death. Women were encouraged to do their 'duty' as mothers, repopulating France. Yet the war years brought severe shortages and threatened Vichy's idealized image of the family. State benefits were not sufficient to feed a growing family, particularly when the main breadwinner was away as a prisoner of war. Despite its promises, the Vichy authorities failed to provide for families. One example was their attitude towards women's paid employment. In October 1940, in its campaign to return women to the home, the regime introduced legislation forbidding certain categories of married women from working in the public sector. By late 1942, this law was revoked as the continued absence of men of working age and the demands of the German occupier meant women were a valuable proportion of the workforce. As with many other aspects of Vichy's National Revolution, plans for a reordered society clashed with the practical realities of a war economy, thus undermining the very ideals the Vichy authorities claimed to support.

Work

With the family as the primary unit of a renewed social order, it was also considered vital to reorganize working lives. Vichy associated urban workers with international Communism and the left-wing ideals of the Popular Front government. Early Vichy legislation, enshrined in the Work Charter of 1941, imposed new working relations. Trade unions were disbanded and owners, managers and workers were made to work together in professional groupings under the supervision of state administrators. The pre-war emphasis on industry and the proletariat was replaced with a nostalgic yearning for rural life and a return to the land. By focusing on rosy images of the *paysan* (rural worker), the regime demonstrated its wish to turn the clock back and to reject modernization.

In reality, France's industrial capacity was key to the German war effort. German demands for food, armaments and primary materials, such as iron and steel, forced the French economy into ever closer collaboration with Nazi Germany. By the end of 1942, Germany had mobilized all the resources of its occupied territories, including France, for its war effort. In February 1943, the Vichy government introduced the *service du travail obligatoire* (forced labour scheme, STO), as Germany demanded two million French workers to boost its faltering war economy. Nearly 650,000 French workers were sent to work in German factories, often against their will. This policy soon backfired as young men, avoiding the call-up to work in Germany, were recruited into the Resistance often in the form of the *maquis*. These were groups of young men on the run from the authorities who hid out in the hills and the mountains. Ultimately, Vichy's romantic views of worker cooperation and a rural idyll masked the real business of economic collaboration with the Germans and its consequences.

Homeland

For those considered to be 'foreign' elements in France, such as Jews, gypsies, freemasons, Communists and homosexuals, Vichy's extremist tendencies were clear from the outset. 'Patrie' or homeland for the Vichy regime was a rejection of Republican views of France as a society of citizens who were equal before the law. Instead, the Vichy regime defined French society in terms of insiders and outsiders. Those who either did not share its political goals, such as

Communists, or did not conform to vague racial criteria, such as Jews and gypsies, were to be excluded from society. The most prominent group among these was the Jews.

In July 1940, Jews who had taken up French nationality since 1927 were stripped of their citizenship. This exposed those who had fled persecution from countries such as Germany, Poland and Romania to the immediate threat of deportation. Vichy introduced Jewish statutes in October 1940 and July 1941. This was discriminatory legislation that targeted Jews for special treatment. They were barred from certain professions and had property and businesses confiscated. Jews' daily lives were further restricted as they were banned from public spaces, such as the local libraries, and forced to travel in segregated carriages of the *métro*. The Germans did not impose these laws. They were the product of anti-Semitic decision-making by French politicians and bureaucrats at Vichy that complemented Nazi ideology.

From 1942, this policy of exclusion was transformed into one of active persecution. French policemen, civil servants and politicians collaborated in the Final Solution, the euphemistic term coined by the Nazis to refer to the extermination of between five and six million Jews living in Europe. In July 1942, after having previously targeted immigrant Jewish men, came the first in a series of large-scale arrests with entire Jewish families detained. These house-to-house raids were carried out by French policemen and designed to facilitate the transport of Jews from France to extermination camps in eastern Europe where they would be gassed to death. Special internment camps were in place in France to deal with the increase in Jewish detainees prior to deportation. These camps had been in existence since 1938, opened by the Third Republic to contain the influx of Jewish refugees fleeing fascism. The Vichy regime extended this network and eventually agreed to oversee the management of internment camps in both the Occupied and Southern Zones. Right up until the summer of 1944, convoys of Jews from all over France were sent to extermination camps, registered and processed by Vichy officials.

The Vichy regime is notorious as the first French government to have enshrined anti-Semitism in law. In the early years, the regime imposed its own discriminatory legislation pre-empting German demands. The memory of this homegrown persecution has been hard for French people to accept. Yet anti-Semitism in France did not originate in the war years. It has a long history that goes back to the **Dreyfus** affair of the 1890s and beyond. During the Occupation, it became clear that many French people did not instinctively endorse the democratic and egalitarian principles of a Republican tradition. They were prepared to ignore, if not condone, the actions of those in power at Vichy. How then did the Resistance come to triumph at the end of the war and what were the alternatives it offered to Vichy's right-wing image of France? The last section of this chapter will examine the development of the Resistance, its aims and objectives, as well as its strengths.

Annette Muller: a child's story

On the night of 16 July 1942, nearly 13,000 French and foreign Jews living in Paris were rounded up and deported to death camps in eastern Europe. This event became known as the round-up of the Vélodrome d'Hiver, named after the sports stadium where Jews were held before being sent to internment camps in preparation for deportation. One of the children caught in this round-up was 9-year-old **Annette Muller** and her brother Michel. On that night, it was French policemen, and not Germans, who arrested mainly women and children, like the Mullers, in an atmosphere of chaos and confusion. Over 4,000 children, some as young as two, were arrested that night. They were separated from their parents in the following days, loaded on to cattle trucks and gassed on arrival at death camps such as Auschwitz. A total of 76,000 Jews were deported from France during the Occupation; only 2,500 survived.

There was a happy ending to Annette Muller's story. Her father bribed an official to have both herself and Michel released from the detention centre where they were awaiting deportation. They were hidden in a Catholic orphanage under assumed identities until the war's end. However, in Annette Muller's autobiographical account of the early years of the war, *La petite fille du Vél d'Hiv* (1991), the childhood narrator returns obsessively to images of her mother, Rachel, and to a little boy, Henri, whom she met in the Vélodrome d'Hiver stadium. Both were deported, never to return. Their memories remain a traumatic reminder of how much individual loss and human suffering lie behind the chilling statistics of French collaboration in the Nazi genocide.

THE RESISTANCE: THE BEGINNINGS

Wartime resistance to the German occupier and the Vichy authorities remains the most positive legacy of the war years. The men and women who risked their lives for the liberation of France have been remembered as great patriots. Yet the defeat of Nazi Germany seemed a faint hope in the early days. For those few French people who refused to accept the armistice with the Germans in June 1940, resistance began tentatively. Some left France to coordinate resistance from abroad from countries such as Great Britain and the USA. In France itself, those who remained met with friends and relatives to discuss events but they had little sense of what they could achieve. With the German invasion of northern France and the collaboration of the Vichy government in the Southern Zone, resistance within France was initially fragmented and localized. It was aimed mainly at countering the propaganda of the authorities, as well as spreading news and information heard from banned sources such as BBC Radio.

In exile in London, General Charles de Gaulle broadcast his famous speech on 18 June 1940 calling on French people to join the Resistance cause (see Extract 6.1 at the end of the chapter). This called on all French people to unite with him to crush the enemy and resist the occupation of France. De Gaulle's appeal was deliberately calculated to be as all-encompassing as possible and did not name the Vichy government as collaborators and traitors. It looked forward to a global war that would see France at the victory table if French men and women chose to engage on the side of the free world. Although few actually heard this appeal, de Gaulle and the Free French organization he founded came to symbolize the Resistance struggle for many within France and abroad.

In order to coordinate the activities of Resistance networks and movements within France and the Free French, de Gaulle parachuted an envoy, **Jean Moulin,** into France in 1943. Moulin's brief was to establish contact with the internal Resistance and to unify the diverse movements in preparation for Allied landings. His crowning achievement before his arrest, torture and death was the creation of the *Conseil National de la Résistance* (National Resistance Committee), which brought together representatives of the major resistance movements and clandestine political parties. At this stage, a sophisticated network of resistance organizations began to emerge which had the potential to be a real threat to the Vichy and German authorities.

VALUES AND IDEALS

Although Vichy propaganda portrayed resisters as bands of social misfits and terrorists, they were generally well-integrated French people. Three major factors motivated people's allegiance to the Resistance. First, many early resisters acted out of patriotism. Anti-German feeling was high as people remembered France's historic defeats at the hands of Germany. Second, people joined the Resistance who had already been involved in the inter-war fight against fascism and had seen its consequences, for example, during the Spanish Civil War. Finally, many rallied to the Resistance from a sense of outrage at the abuse of individual rights under the Occupation. A belief in the values of liberty, equality and fraternity moved many to defend what they saw as Republican traditions and values.

The primary aim of the Resistance was national liberation. However, freedom was not construed solely in terms of ridding France of its invader. The Occupation of France was about more than territorial invasion. It had involved the loss of basic rights, such as freedom of expression, which French people had come to associate with living under a democracy. Clandestine resistance propaganda emphasized the censorship exercised by German and

Vichy authorities. The occupying authorities seized over two million books deemed to be either critical of Nazi Germany or contrary to National Socialism. Over 850 writers and translators were banned, mostly due to their Jewish origins or left-wing affiliations. Even classical French authors and playwrights were censored if they were perceived to promote resistance to oppression. This censorship was more than the mere control of information. It represented a sustained attack on French culture as the repository of ideals and values that could bolster resisters. Indeed, for many clandestine writers and activists, those who published legally under such conditions were betraying not only the Resistance but also their own country. In its propaganda battle against the Vichy regime, the Resistance understood the importance of language both as a weapon of war and as a means of defending its vision of a liberated France and its democratic Republican heritage.

UNITY IN DIVERSITY

By 1943, the Resistance in France had developed to incorporate many activities designed to combat the German invader and to undermine Vichy propaganda. Clandestine newspapers circulated Allied news and boosted morale. Intelligence networks sent back information on German installations and French industrial capacity to Allied command. Specialist networks helped Jews, stranded Allied airmen and other groups sought by the Germans and Vichy to escape. Much of this activity involved the cooperation of people who were not associated with politics at the time, such as women, or those who had previously been at opposing ends of the political spectrum.

French women played an important role in the Resistance, mainly supporting and coordinating local action. French women had still not gained the vote by 1940, despite well-publicized campaigns during the inter-war period, and few had direct experience of political action. However, women excelled as support workers, using the traditional roles of housewife and mother as a cover for subversive activities. Often chosen as liaison agents, they distributed information, arms and equipment at the risk of their lives. Women were suited to this role as contact points because they were able to fade into the background more easily than men, especially after the introduction of the forced labour scheme in 1943. Such women became vital to the infrastructure of their resistance movements and a very few even acceded to positions of major responsibility. Equally, groups worked together who had traditionally been enemies. Jewish immigrants from eastern Europe, Spanish Republicans fleeing the Franco regime and French Communists fought in alliance with more conservative groups and personalities, such as **Henri Frenay**, ex-army officer and leader of *Combat*, one of the largest resistance movements in the south of France. Relations were fraught, particularly over the distribution of weapons and the reorganization of post-war France. However, compromises were reached in the common goal of national liberation and, overall, the diversity of the Resistance was a great asset in its struggle.

LIBERATION

The Liberation of France was long and bloody. It began on 6 June 1944 with D-Day and Allied landings on beaches in Normandy. The combined forces of the internal Resistance were mobilized to work in tandem with the Allied armies. *Maquis* groups disrupted communications networks and sabotaged German troop movements. Resistance forces engaged in skirmishes with French paramilitary groups loyal to Vichy and suffered tragic if courageous defeats in the mountains of Glières and Vercors. Retreating German forces exacted horrific reprisals on communities suspected of harbouring or aiding resisters, such as the shooting and burning of over 600 villagers at Oradour-sur Glâne. Eventually, on 25 August 1944, French forces liberated Paris and de Gaulle walked in triumph down the Champs Élysées, acclaimed by the crowds.

Yet there was a downside to this image of French triumph. From June to November 1944, nearly 9,000 suspected collaborators were executed for war crimes with no legal trial or representation. Personal vendettas and collective frustrations erupted into spectacular action, including the public head-shaving of women accused of denouncing resisters or having relationships with German soldiers. This period of bloodletting was likened to an undeclared civil war. In a second phase, a further 1,500 executions and 45,000 prison sentences were carried out, this time sanctioned by the provisional government of France, headed by de Gaulle. By 1958, all but 19 of those imprisoned for war crimes had been freed under a series of amnesties. However, this collective pardon could not alter the enduring legacy of the Occupation as a time when French people fought as much among themselves as against the German invader.

CONCLUSION: WARTIME MEMORIES

General de Gaulle's vision of France as a nation of resisters who had bravely ousted the invader played an important part in the reconstruction of France in the immediate post-war period. De Gaulle understood that the country needed a myth of national unity around which a new destiny for France could be forged. The heroism of the Resistance legitimized the founding of the Fourth Republic and many of its leading figures relied on their pedigree as resistance activists. In recent years, historians have challenged de Gaulle's glorious image of France's war record. Studies of French collaboration in the Final Solution and of how ordinary French people 'accommodated' the Germans have damaged national confidence. Even today, French people continue to question and judge the behaviour of those who lived under the Occupation.

In 1997, the trial of former Vichy civil servant, **Maurice Papon,** for crimes against humanity reopened old wounds. Papon was tried for his role as a regional administrator who oversaw the arrest and deportation of Jews from the Bordeaux region to the transit centre of Drancy in Paris between 1942 and 1944. Condemning Papon to ten years' imprisonment, the verdict of the French court recognized the crimes of the Vichy regime. Yet many felt that the trial had come too late and that the verdict was a fudge of the most basic questions concerning French state responsibility for crimes against humanity. Papon's post-war career as a high-ranking government official muddied the waters still further. While Paris Police Chief in 1961, Papon directed the violent police suppression of a peaceful demonstration by Algerians supporting independence for the then French colony. This event, brought to the fore by his 1997 trial, led many French people to ponder not so much the differences between the Vichy regime and the French Republic but the continuity in some of their policing methods and attitudes towards immigrants.

This chapter has shown how the war years constituted a moment of unparalleled conflict for French people. France would experience divisions again over the loss of its colonies in the 1950s and 1960s and face the riots and strikes of May 1968. Yet, the Second World War tested French people's commitment to a democratic form of government like no other period. In terms of French history, the war years ushered in major changes. Women voted for the first time in municipal elections in October 1945, at last fully-fledged citizens of the French Republic. The next three decades were named *les trente glorieuses* (the 30 glorious years) in celebration of France's great economic expansion. Nonetheless, the experiment of the Vichy regime revealed how fragile the Republican ideals of liberty, equality, fraternity could be in times of crisis. Although the Republic would reassert itself in 1946 with the founding of the Fourth Republic, the Occupation highlighted the continuing presence of right-wing elements in French political life ready to profit from its demise. In 1949, Louis Mornet, the French public prosecutor in the post-war trial of Pétain, entitled his Occupation memoirs *Quatre ans à rayer de notre histoire* (Four years to erase from our history). Many French Republicans then and since have agreed with his sentiments.

Extract 6.1: General Charles de Gaulle's radio appeal from London to the French people, 18 June 1940

Français, Françaises!

Les chefs qui, depuis de nombreuses années, sont à la tête des armées, ont formé un gouvernement.

Ce gouvernement, alléguant la défaite de nos armées, s'est mis en rapport avec l'ennemi pour cesser le combat.

Certes, nous avons été, nous sommes, submergés par la force mécanique, terrestre et aérienne, de l'ennemi.

Infiniment plus que leur nombre, ce sont les chars, les avions, la tactique des Allemands qui nous font reculer. Ce sont les chars, les avions, la tactique des Allemands qui ont surpris nos chefs au point de les amener là où ils en sont aujourd'hui.

Mais le dernier mot est-il dit? L'espérance doit-elle disparaître? La défaite est-elle définitive? Non!

Croyez-moi, moi qui vous parle en connaissance de cause et vous dis que rien n'est perdu pour la France. Les mêmes moyens qui ont vaincus peuvent faire venir un jour la victoire.

Car la France n'est pas seule! Elle n'est pas seule! Elle a un vaste Empire derrière elle. Elle peut faire bloc avec l'Empire britannique qui tient la mer et qui continue la lutte. Elle peut, comme l'Angleterre, utiliser sans limites l'immense industrie des États-Unis.

Cette guerre n'est pas limitée au territoire malheureux de notre pays. Cette guerre n'est pas tranchée par la bataille de France. Cette guerre est une guerre mondiale. Toutes les fautes, tous les retards, toutes les souffrances n'empêchent pas qu'il y a, dans l'univers, tous les moyens nécessaires pour écraser un jour nos ennemis. . . .

Moi, Général de Gaulle, actuellement à Londres, j'invite les officiers et les soldats français qui se trouvent en territoire britannique ou qui viendraient à s'y trouver, avec leurs armes ou sans leurs armes, j'invite les ingénieurs et les ouvriers spécialistes des industries d'armement qui se trouvent en territoire britannique ou qui viendraient à s'y trouver, à se mettre en rapport avec moi.

Quoi qu'il arrive, la flamme de la résistance française ne doit pas s'éteindre et ne s'étreindra pas.

Source: Colin Nettelbeck, 1994: *War and identity: the French and the Second World War*. London: Routledge, pp. 24 and 26

Frenchmen and Frenchwomen!

Those who have led our French armies for many years have formed a government.

Invoking the defeat of our armies, this government has contacted the enemy in order to end the struggle.

It is true that we have been, we are, overwhelmed by the technical power of the enemy on land and in the air.

Much more significant than their numbers, it is the tanks, the planes and the strategy of the Germans that cause us to retreat. It is the tanks, the planes and the strategy of the Germans that have so surprised our leaders as to bring them to where they are today.

But has the last word been had? Must all hope disappear? Is it defeat once and for all? No!

As one who speaks to you fully aware of the facts, believe me when I tell you that all is not lost for France. The same means that defeated us can one day bring about victory.

Because France is not alone! She is not alone! She has a vast empire behind her. She can make common cause with the British empire which rules the seas and carries on the struggle. Like England, she can make limitless use of the great industrial resources of the United States.

This war is not limited to the unfortunate land of our country. This war has not been decided by the battle for France. This war is a world war. All the errors, all the delays, all the suffering cannot prevent the fact that, in this universe, all the necessary means exist to crush our enemies one day. . . .

I, General de Gaulle, currently in London, I invite all officers and French soldiers who are presently on British soil or who should find themselves here, with or without their weapons, I invite all engineers and trained workers from the armaments industry who are presently on British soil or should find themselves here, to contact me.

Whatever happens, the flame of the resistance must not and will never be extinguished.

FURTHER READING

Jackson, J. 2001. *France: the dark years*. Oxford: Oxford University Press.
Comprehensive history of the Occupation from its origins in the inter-war period to post-war legacies and memories.

Kedward, H. R. 1985. *Occupied France: resistance and collaboration*. Oxford: Blackwell.
Excellent general study of developments during the war.

Rousso, H. 1992. *Les années noires: vivre sous l'occupation*. Paris: Gallimard.
Concise overview of France during the war years with illustrations and an appendix of extracts from diaries and letters.

7

The Brazzaville Conference of 1944: the dream of a greater French Republic

Gordon Cumming

INTRODUCTION

On the eve of the Second World War, France controlled a vast colonial empire which included territories in Africa, Asia, Latin America, the Caribbean and the Pacific. At the same time as possessing this empire, however, France was also a Republic with a constitutional commitment to values such as freedom, equality and fraternity. On the face of it, France's imperial ambitions were incompatible with the country's Republican ideals. Yet French governments did not see any inconsistency between the two and did not feel the need to 'justify' the existence of France's empire until the time of the Second World War and the now legendary Brazzaville Conference of 1944. This chapter will focus on the events and implications of this conference and will examine how far it challenged or confirmed French assumptions about the compatibility of empire and Republic.

THE ORIGINS OF THE REPUBLICAN DREAM

Before examining the significance of the Brazzaville Conference, it is worth asking how French governments justified their administration of an empire whose very structure and existence seemed to betray the values of equality and fraternity laid down in the 1789 Declaration of the Rights of Man and the Citizen. The answer is that successive French governments argued that the colonial empire was simply a prelude to the creation of *une République de 100 millions de Français* (a Republic of 100 million Frenchmen). This Republic of 100 million Frenchmen would include not only the citizens of metropolitan France, but also all the peoples of *La France d'Outre Mer* (Overseas France). The eventual establishment of this *Plus Grande France* (Greater French Republic) would be achieved through France's *mission civilisatrice* (civilizing mission) which would give the native populations in France's colonies the benefit of 'superior' French civilization, culture and language. Officials argued that this civilizing mission would bring an end to the 'uncivilized' practices they regarded as characteristic of the colonies: cannibalism, slave-trading, human sacrifice and witchcraft. Moreover, it would, they claimed, institute a process of *assimilation*, through which colonial subjects could gradually be assimilated culturally, legally and politically into the French way of life.

France's doctrine of *assimilation* had its origins in the French Revolution. It was based upon the thinking of philosophers who believed that education could achieve equality across races and individuals. Yet, while *assimilation* was usually understood in abstract terms, it was not an empty concept. The first clear statement of France's intention to assimilate colonial peoples came in 1794 when the leaders of the French Revolution abolished slavery and declared that all men, without distinction as to colour, who are residents of the colonies, were French citizens. In 1795, the new French Constitution affirmed that the colonies were integral parts of the Republic, subject to the same constitutional laws. While **Napoléon Bonaparte** subsequently annulled these provisions in 1802, they were not the last attempt to marry Republicanism and colonialism. Thus, after the 1848 revolution, the French Second Republic turned Algeria into an outlying 'district' of the French Republic and conferred French citizenship on all the inhabitants of the 'old colonies' (that is, Martinique, Guadeloupe, French Guyana, Réunion Island and the Four Communes of Senegal). These citizens' rights were eroded under France's authoritarian Second Empire, but later decrees did further the rights of native populations in the colonies. Thus the Crémieux declaration of 1870 allowed the naturalization of the Jewish population within Algeria. The *Loi Diagne* (Diagne Law) of 1916 enabled the inhabitants of the Four Communes of Senegal to remain French citizens without giving up their religious customs; and the Jonnart reforms of 1919 granted French citizenship to Algerians who agreed to 'live like Frenchmen'.

France's willingness to assimilate colonized peoples or to grant them citizenship must not be overstated, however. The fact is that citizenship was only accorded to a handful of 'old colonies' under French control. And, even here, citizens' rights were under constant threat. White settlers in these colonies objected to the extension of rights to 'natives' (the French settlers known as *pieds noirs* in Algeria blocked legislation in the late 1930s to extend the vote to more Algerian Muslims). Moreover, authoritarian figures such as **Marshal Pétain** quashed freedoms and reintroduced racial discrimination in France's Vichy-occupied colonies in the early 1940s.

As mainstream Republicanism in France moved away from its revolutionary idealism from the 1880s onwards, it moved away too from the idea that French citizenship could be obtained simply through an act of will. More stringent conditions were introduced by which access to French citizenship was restricted. In particular, France required colonial subjects to support themselves financially and to be at least 21; to have served three years in the French public service or military; to be well educated in French and to live according to the French civil code. This latter condition was particularly difficult for Muslims to fulfil, for it required religious observance to be restricted to private life. Such a restriction denied some of the fundamental tenets of Islam, and Muslims risked becoming outcasts from their own society.

Significantly, too, France simply did not accord citizenship to the majority of her colonial 'subjects', since access to citizenship was only accorded in the 'old colonies' under French control. Elsewhere, people were required to accept a form of colonial rule that had nothing to do with the 1789 Declaration of the Rights of Man that emphatically states, 'Men are born and live free and equal in rights.' These peoples did not benefit from democratic freedoms; instead they were ruled by decrees from France and given virtually no say in colonial affairs. They did not enjoy equality before the law, but were subject to forced labour, taxation, compulsory military service and the *indigénat* (the legal code which allowed French administrators to impose summary penalties on 'troublesome natives').

Despite the wide discrepancy between the rhetoric of *assimilation* and the reality of colonial practice, the dream of a Greater French Republic persisted and went virtually unchallenged right up to the Second World War. It was initially defended most vociferously by the Republican Left. The Left often took the view that colonies were a demonstration of the universal character of the French Republican model and of Republican principles, for the colonies showed that Republicanism could be applied everywhere, regardless of social and cultural distinctions. But the ideal of *La France d'Outre Mer* also came to be endorsed by the political Right, who saw in it a remnant of the greatness and privileges of France's monarchical past.

There were, of course, plenty of people who could see and who were prepared to expose the incompatibility between colonial domination and Republican values. These critics included prominent intellectuals such as **André Gide** who shocked the French public with his 1927 account of forced labour in Equatorial Africa, *Voyage au Congo* (Voyage to the Congo). Organized indigenous agitation for freedom came from nationalist movements in North Africa, Indo-China and parts of Sub-Saharan Africa. The French Communist Party, a powerful influence in mid-twentieth-century France, demanded an end to imperialism as a whole, seeing it as the geographical extension of capitalism. And a different type of concern was voiced by French colonial administrators who were often sceptical about the real prospects and point of *assimilation*, particularly in Sub-Saharan Africa where the 'natives' were considered too brutish to be improved and where living conditions were never likely to attract many French settlers. These administrators espoused an alternative doctrine known as *association*, contending that French governments should delegate some powers to colonial peoples and should respect their customs rather than trying to incorporate them into French Republican institutions and values systems.

Significantly, however, these opposition voices were either unable to, or simply did not wish to, put a stop to French colonial rule. In the case of Gide and other similarly concerned intellectuals, they did not call for the end of the colonial system, simply the end of 'abuses' within this system. As for nationalist movements, these were mostly (with the exception of Indo-China, which rebelled in 1930) embryonic, non-violent and, for the most part, not especially radical. The French Communists, for their part, did call for uprisings in the colonies but their true focus was on fomenting worker revolution in the industrialized, capitalist West. Finally, although colonial administrators favoured *association* in their day-to-day dealings on the ground with colonized peoples, in their rhetoric they clung tenaciously to the principle of *assimilation* and to the dream of a Greater French Republic.

BRAZZAVILLE: A TIME FOR REFLECTION

The Brazzaville Conference was held in the capital of the French Congo from 30 January to 8 February 1944. It had been convened by the leader of the Free French, General **Charles de Gaulle**, and was soon to acquire legendary significance as a major turning point in French colonial politics. It is sometimes viewed as the first move towards France's eventual withdrawal from its colonies, and as the key moment when true Republican values triumphed over imperial ambitions.

There is some evidence to support this reading of the conference. To begin with, Brazzaville did mark a watershed, insofar as it opened up to international scrutiny the whole debate about empire and its future relationship to the French Republic. For the conference was held in a semi-public forum, with members of the press in attendance alongside consular representatives from Britain, Belgium and from the contemporary arch-critic of colonialism, the United States. There was, as such, unprecedented pressure on the French administration to live up to its Republican ideals and to demonstrate that the government of post-war France would follow a more enlightened policy towards the colonies than the prejudiced Vichy regime had done.

Furthermore, Brazzaville did allow for discussion of the relative merits of the practices of *association* and *assimilation,* as well as debate about a possible federal structure linking France to her African colonies. Following these discussions, the conference recommended that colonized peoples should be given a large measure of freedom; that they should eventually 'be associated with the management of public affairs in their country'; and that they should be encouraged to create their own political identity or 'personality'.

Finally, the conference was also critical of France's unRepublican practices in the colonies. It set out to reward colonized peoples for their loyalty during the war and to bring French policy into line with the principles of liberty, equality and fraternity. To this end, Brazzaville proposed an end to forced labour, the abolition of the *indigénat* (the discriminatory legal code applied to 'natives'), and improved access to social, health and education provision. It also recommended that Africans should have the right to form trade unions, to vote in local assemblies, and to elect representatives to the Constituent Assembly which would be formed after the war to draw up the Constitution of the Fourth Republic. This latter 'privilege' was continued throughout the Fourth Republic (1946–58) and it gave African *députés* the right to sit in the French Parliament, to affiliate their political groupings to French parties and to shame France into liberalizing her policy towards the colonies.

Overall, it is clear that the Brazzaville Conference did propose some bold reforms which, if taken to their logical conclusion, could have led to the end of the French empire. However, Brazzaville involved only a limited assertion of the Republican egalitarian spirit and did not reflect a desire to grant complete autonomy to colonized peoples. For the conference was primarily concerned with preserving France's empire which, after the humiliation of defeat in 1940, was perceived as absolutely vital to her identity as a great power.

That Brazzaville was not truly a moment of triumph for French Republican values can be inferred from its list of participants. The conference was attended by some 44 French colonial administrators, political and trade union leaders, most of whom were better suited to dealing with day-to-day administrative questions than they were to defining a long-term policy. There was, moreover, only one black representative present and he was not there in his capacity as an African under French rule, but as the Governor-General of French Equatorial Africa. That the conference was not revolutionary can also be seen in the fact that its delegates ultimately rejected *association* in favour of *assimilation*. They also opposed any restructuring of the colonies that might eventually lead to independence. This opposition was clearly enunciated in the opening speech by de Gaulle's Commissioner of Colonies (see Extract 7.1). And the document produced at the end of the conference affirmed that the French colonies would always belong to France and that self-government was absolutely excluded, even as a future possibility.

A further sign of conservatism can be detected in the way that all of Brazzaville's recommendations were heavily qualified. Thus, for example, the conference advocated the abolition of forced labour but allowed five years for this to be phased out. It also suggested that Africans should have access to public service posts but not to the highest grades. Furthermore, it recommended greater provision for education in French – native languages were banned from schools – but shied away from advocating the level of investment required to turn France's assimilationist dream into reality. Finally, the conference used the fact that it was only an advisory forum to sidestep constitutional questions relating to African representation in the French Parliament. In so doing, it allowed French policy-makers in the post-war governments to introduce a dual-college electoral system where greater weight was given to the votes of French expatriates in the colonies than to the votes of the indigenous people.

AFTER BRAZZAVILLE: A RUDE AWAKENING

It follows that Brazzaville was largely a stage-managed affair whose recommendations were marked by ambiguity and open to diverse interpretations. It was partly the vagueness and partly the timing (just before the end of the war) of Brazzaville's recommendations which ensured that they did not face any organized resistance and which helped them to form the basis of an unprecedented consensus on colonial issues. This consensus included the French public and political establishment which welcomed the Brazzaville proposals as a way of colonizing and liberalizing at the same time; and which naïvely assumed that the loyalty of France's colonized subjects during the war proved that France's civilizing mission was working and should be continued.

But while Brazzaville's vaguely reformist proposals were enough to satisfy political leaders in France and the small elite of Africans who had become assimilated to French culture, they seemed outmoded and timid in a post-war era that cried out for radical new thinking. The conference simply did not go far enough to silence critics. In the international community, as well as in France and in the French colonies, many questioned whether French officials had any serious intention of bringing the Republican values of liberty, equality and fraternity to her colonial peoples. And many questioned further whether France should even be trying to impose the French Republican model on these peoples.

THE INTERNATIONAL COMMUNITY: COMPETING VISIONS OF REPUBLICANISM

The international community was generally hostile to the model of continued colonial rule proposed at Brazzaville, and sceptical about France's claim to be creating a Greater French Republic. The most vociferous critic was the United States. Conscious of its own colonial past and of the minority Afro-American population in its midst, the USA had long been keen to see African peoples progress towards self-government. During the war this anti-colonial sentiment increased, and America drew up the Atlantic Charter of 1941 which set out as a war aim of the Allies that they should respect the right of all peoples to choose the form of government under which they live. The American President, Franklin D. Roosevelt, insisted that this Charter applied to colonized peoples everywhere, and his administration even stimulated nationalist sentiment in parts of France's empire. Roosevelt was in effect offering the world the American model of Republicanism, based on freedom and other 'inalienable rights' within a multiracial society (or 'melting pot'). He was, at the same time, challenging the validity of France's Republican model which sought to impose a uniform secular system on colonized peoples, whether they wanted it or not. He was shocked by France's refusal to liberate her colonies, and by France's seeming arrogance in refusing to acknowledge that the international community had any valid interest in the way that French colonies were run.

The USA was not the only country opposed to French colonialism. The other superpower, Soviet Russia, was also a vociferous opponent of European imperialism. Soviet Russia saw French and other colonies as much-needed outlets for capitalist economies and therefore as obstacles to the workers' revolution which would overthrow Western imperialism and allow the establishment of Marxist republics based not so much on civil and political liberties as on economic and social equality.

After the superpowers, the next most ardent critic of colonialism was the United Nations which expounded, in Article 73 of its Charter, the need to help colonized peoples develop self-government. Throughout the post-war years, the UN would voice the views of many countries opposed to colonialism, not least those states which had already gained independence from their former colonizers, countries such as India (colonized by Britain), Indonesia (colonized by The Netherlands), and Syria (colonized by the French).

OPPOSITION IN FRANCE: A BETRAYAL OF THE REPUBLIC

In France, there was initially little opposition to the Brazzaville proposals, not least since the conference had been portrayed by imperial propagandists as a symbol of France's modern and reforming colonial spirit (the *esprit de Brazzaville*). But opposition grew as the return to colonial rule became a reality and as several colonial wars, where indigenous peoples challenged French administration, shook the ruling class's certainties about France's assimilationist dream.

Protest within France came primarily from the French Left and from intellectuals living in France in the post-war period. The main opponents on the Left were the Socialists and the Communists. The Socialists soon began to lose confidence in the ideal of *assimilation*. They came to recognize that the extension of liberty and equality to non-European people could not be accomplished by simply treating them as notional French citizens. They should be equal in all rights, but they might also be different. They should be able to choose to adopt a French identity, but free to accept or reject French civilization – or to accept parts of it and reject others.

The French Communist Party, especially after it had been expelled from government in 1947, adopted an extremely critical stance against French imperialism. Broadly realigning itself with the policy and rhetoric in Soviet Russia, the French Communist Party spoke out against colonialism in the French National Assembly. It encouraged Africans to set up study groups, trade unions and mass political parties, and urged them to break free from the political and cultural constraints of France's 'One and Indivisible' Republic.

The French Left found natural allies among African and West Indian intellectuals and politicians living in France in the post-war period. One of the most prominent of these figures was the Senegalese poet and politician, **Léopold Sédar Senghor**. Senghor sought, in critically acclaimed poetry collections like *Chants d'ombre* (1945) (*Shadow songs*), to promote the idea of *négritude*, that is, the notion that there are essential African characteristics (such as sensuality, rhythm, emotion) diametrically opposed to essential European characteristics (such as logic, reasoning, intellectualism). Senghor saw black African culture as having retained an authentic beauty and spontaneity which 'rational' European cultures have now lost. He rejected the idea that African colonies should be 'assimilated' into the dominant French Republican, cultural and linguistic model. He argued instead that *assimilation* should be a two-way process and should lead to a form of *métissage* ('hybridity'), whereby 'Black' and 'European' identities would create a new 'mixed' culture.

A more radical critic of colonialism was **Aimé Césaire**, the French West Indian poet, playwright and politician. A co-founder of the *négritude* movement, Césaire was unrelenting in his attack on European countries like France which used fine words to defend a brutal, racist, and potentially even fascist policy of colonial rule. He challenged France to examine how Republican it truly was by arguing, in his celebrated *Discours sur le colonialisme* (1955) (*Discourse on colonialism*), that any 'civilization' which could defend colonialism – the domination of one people by another – was fundamentally morally sick (see Extract 7.2).

Crucially, Césaire and Senghor enjoyed the support of French intellectuals like long-time Marxist and existentialist **Jean-Paul Sartre**. Nicknamed 'the Pope of the anti-colonial movement' (*le pape de l'anti-colonialisme*), Sartre viewed French imperialism as an affront to Republican values and a scandal given that France was herself only just emerging from a period of German Occupation. He drew attention to the plight of colonial peoples through his work as joint editor of the radical journal *Les Temps Modernes*; through his support for the first black African journal, *Présence Africaine*; and through his now-famous preface to Senghor's 1948 *Anthology of new black poetry*. Sartre went further in the 1950s, campaigning vigorously against

France's colonial wars in Indo-China and Algeria and urging the violent overthrow of Western imperialism.

THE EMPIRE STRIKES BACK

The other source of opposition to the Brazzaville proposals for continued colonial rule came from within France's empire itself. This opposition was largely muted in Sub-Saharan Africa, where culturally assimilated leaders generally wanted to see France complete her civilizing mission and where large-scale violent protests – such as the uprising against French colonialism which happened in Madagascar in 1947 – never really became the main mode of dealing with the French authorities.

More radical opposition to French rule came from Indo-China and Algeria. The former was considered 'off-limits' at Brazzaville, largely because it was in the hands of the Vichy regime and the Japanese towards the end of the war. The conference did, nonetheless, find ways of including Indo-China in its discussions and, by implication, its recommendations. Thus, for example, Brazzaville began with a pious statement of solidarity to 'captive Indo-China'. Significantly, too, the opening speech by de Gaulle implied that the conference would be concerned with the future of the whole empire. He suggested that it would seek 'to choose nobly, liberally, the way of a new era in which to direct the sixty million people who find themselves associated with the destiny of her [France's] forty-two million children'.

But the idea that the Brazzaville Conference proposals were to provide an overall blueprint for France's empire was alarming to Indo-China. As France's richest and most populous colonial possession, with a proud cultural and linguistic heritage that French colonialism had not succeeded in suppressing, Indo-China was simply not willing to see its identity submerged within a uniform, secular French Republic. It rejected France's offer of special privileges (such as semi-autonomy, dual French and Indo-Chinese citizenship) and strongly resisted French attempts at recolonization. The Indo-Chinese war that ensued in 1946–54 showed France to be the colonial aggressor and seriously undermined belief in the extent to which the French Republic wished to apply Republican principles in its colonies.

As for Algeria, this territory was also not openly discussed at Brazzaville, and references to it were in fact struck from the record of the conference. Algeria's concern was that Brazzaville's assimilationist proposals would be applied to North Africa. The fact that the Algerian Governor-General had been invited to observe the conference proceedings seemed to suggest that this was France's intention. So too did de Gaulle's announcement, only a few weeks after Brazzaville, of plans to assimilate and give the vote to tens of thousands of Algerian Muslims.

It goes without saying that *assimilation* was no more acceptable to the

Algerian people, who had their own religion, laws and languages, than it was to the Indo-Chinese. Algerian critics of French colonialism had been calling for autonomy since before the war and their non-violent opposition to colonial rule had intensified during the war as they witnessed France's humiliating defeat and as they gained support from the United States. Algerian nationalists opposed French plans to reimpose a secular Republican model, and, in 1945, showed the first sign of violent resistance in the eastern Algerian town of Sétif. The brutal repression of this uprising was to foreshadow France's bloody eight-year war with Algeria (1954–62) against Algerian independence.

More than any other overseas event, the Algerian War was to shake the foundations of the French Fourth Republic, both as an ideal and as an institution. Even today, its legacy is bitterly contested. It exposed a whole generation of French men to the brutality of war and to the sight of torture and summary executions. It provoked massive criticism from French intellectuals including establishment figures like **François Mauriac** who sought to shame the French public into speaking out against France's unRepublican actions in Algeria. It also dealt a near-fatal blow to France's image of herself as a Republican country founded on the ideals contained in the Declaration of the Rights of Man. It led to the moral and political collapse of the Fourth Republic and resulted in the founding of a new (Fifth) Republic under Charles de Gaulle.

CONCLUSION: THE DREAM LIVES ON

This chapter has shown how, for many years, France rationalized its imperial practices through Republican rhetoric. It has demonstrated how French governments, despite the racist nature of French colonial rule, had hardly needed to 'defend' the existence of the empire until the time of the Brazzaville Conference.

Brazzaville held out the prospect of radical change but was ultimately a conservative affair whose proposals for continued imperial rule failed to satisfy international, national and colonial critics. Eventually these anti-colonial forces became so powerful that France was forced to give up Indo-China and Algeria and, with these territories, her dream of a Greater French Republic, 'One and Indivisible'. France's relations with Indo-China were severed for over three decades. In the aftermath of the Algerian War, ties with Algeria came to be marked by flows of immigration into France, which have brought new challenges and demonstrated the enduring nature of French *assimilationiste* (assimilationist) policies. France has tried hard to assimilate, or rather 'integrate', large Muslim communities into the secular Republic at the same time as containing rising levels of racism. The extreme difficulty of achieving this was reflected most alarmingly in the 2002 French Presidential elections in which the anti-immigration National Front Party candidate, **Jean-Marie Le Pen**, came second.

Yet, in other parts of the former empire, France has faced much less opposition and has had scope to continue with the grand project of *assimilation* into a Greater French Republic. A number of France's 'old colonies' – now called *Départements et Territoires d'Outre-Mer* (Overseas Departments and Territories or DOM TOM) – have been integrated into the French Republic. France has allowed the people of these countries in the South Pacific, the Indian Ocean and the French West Indies to benefit from French citizenship, to vote in French elections, and to enjoy access to the French education and welfare systems.

In Francophone Sub-Saharan Africa too, France has had scope to pursue her dream of *assimilation*, thanks to the largely peaceful way in which independence was achieved in this region. French governments have had to accept that independent African states no longer wish to be part of the indivisible French Republic and that African peoples do not aspire to French citizenship. Yet France has managed to hold on to her ideal of a Greater French Republic simply by repackaging it as a new concept offering new benefits, that of the 'Franco-African family'. France has actively promoted this idea by fostering personal friendships between French and African leaders. It has also done so by adopting an over-indulgent attitude towards rogue members of this 'family' such as Jean-Bedel Bokassa, the self-styled 'Emperor for Life' of the Central African Republic, and President Juvénal Habyarimana, the leader of the Hutu regime, which carried out the 1994 genocide in Rwanda. French governments have further reinforced this sense of 'family' by holding regular gatherings such as the Franco-African summit, where the French President is 'first among equals' in the company of African Heads of State, and the *Francophonie* (French-speaking, or 'Francophone') summits, where 54 French-speaking countries come together to support the spread of the French language. France has, moreover, successfully portrayed herself as head of this 'family' by becoming the largest provider of economic aid, military support and cultural assistance to former French colonies in Africa.

So French governments have clearly been more successful in gaining acceptance of the idea of a Franco-African family than they ever were in selling the idea of a Greater French Republic. There are obvious reasons why this should be the case. Above all, the concept of a 'family of nations' suggests that a special relationship exists between France and its former colonies and that this relationship is based upon common goals and a mutual recognition of the sovereignty and equality of the states involved. The reality is, of course, different: the French have frequently used this idea to preserve their sphere of influence in Africa, to increase African economic dependency on France and to discourage African peoples from forming identities which are not modelled on French cultural and political identities. Only time will tell whether this Franco-African family can continue to exist happily or whether a new generation of African leaders will reject France's continuing influence on the politics and culture of their countries.

Extract 7.1: Statement from the Brazzaville Conference of 1944

C'est l'homme, c'est l'Africain, ce sont ses aspirations, ses besoins, et n'hésitons pas à le reconnaître, ses faiblesses . . . qui seront la préoccupation constante de cette conférence; c'est l'incorporation des masses indigènes dans le monde français, l'évolution de nos liens avec elles, du stade du dévouement instinctif . . . au loyalisme nécessairement différent et plus nuancé de l'éduqué et du citoyen, c'est l'ascension des populations africaines vers la personnalité politique . . . .

Un demi-siècle a suffi à la France pour faire régner sur ces immenses territoires l'ordre et la paix, pour les couvrir des institutions de l'éducation, de l'assistance, de l'apostolat et des réalisations techniques. . . . Nous lisons de temps en temps que cette guerre doit se terminer par . . . un affranchissement des peuples coloniaux. Dans la grande France coloniale, il n'y a ni peuples à affranchir ni discriminations raciales à abolir. Il y a des populations qui se sentent Français et qui veulent prendre . . . une part de plus en plus large dans la vie de la communauté française. Il y a des populations que nous entendons conduire, étape par étape, à la personnalité (politique) . . . mais qui n'entendent connaître d'autre indépendance que l'indépendance de la France.

Source: R. Pleven, 1945: *Conférence Africaine Française, Brazzaville, 30 janvier–8 février 1944*. Paris: Ministère des Colonies, p. 22

It is man and the African, his aspirations and needs, and let us not shy away from acknowledging it, his weaknesses . . . which will be the constant preoccupation of this conference; it is the incorporation of the indigenous masses into the French world, the development of our links with them, from the stage of instinctive devotion . . . to the loyalty of the educated man and citizen, which is necessarily different and more qualified, it is the ascent of African populations towards political identity . . . .

One half-century has been sufficient for France to make order and peace reign over these vast territories, to cover them with the institutions of education, welfare, of proselytism, and with technical accomplishments . . . From time to time we read that this war must end with . . . a freeing of colonial peoples. In greater colonial France, there are neither peoples to be freed nor racial discriminations to be abolished. There are populations who feel themselves to be Frenchmen, and who wish to play . . . a greater part in the life of the French community. There are populations that we want to lead, step by step, to (political) identity . . . but who do not want to know any other independence than that of France.

Extract 7.2: The Martinique poet Aimé Césaire critiquing French colonialism, 1955

Chaque fois qu'il y a au Viêt-nam une tête coupée et un œil crevé et qu'en France on accepte, une fillette violée et qu'en France on accepte, un Malgache supplicié et qu'en France on accepte, il y a un acquis de la civilization qui pèse de son poids mort, une régression universelle qui s'opère, une gangrène qui s'installe, un foyer d'infection qui s'étend. . . . Au bout de cet orgueil racial encouragé, de cette jactance étalée, il y a le poison instillé dans les veines de l'Europe, et le progrès lent, mais sûr, de l'ensauvagement du continent.

. . . Il vaudrait la peine d'étudier, cliniquement, dans les détails, les démarches d'Hitler et de l'hitlérisme de révéler au très distingué, très humaniste, très chrétien bourgeois du XXe siècle qu[e] . . . ce qu'il ne pardonne pas à Hitler, ce n'est pas *le crime* en soi, *le crime contre l'homme*, ce n'est pas *l'humiliation de l'homme en soi*, c'est le crime contre l'homme blanc, c'est l'humiliation de l'homme blanc, et d'avoir appliqué à l'Europe des procédés colonialistes dont ne relevaient jusqu'ici que les Arabes d'Algérie, les coolies de l'Inde et les nègres d'Afrique.

Source: Aimé Cesaire, 1955: *Discours sur le colonialisme*. Paris: Présence Africaine, pp. 11–12

Each time a head is cut off or an eye put out in Vietnam and in France they accept the fact, each time a little girl is raped and in France they accept the fact, each time a Madagascan is tortured and in France they accept the fact, civilization acquires another dead weight, a universal regression takes place, a gangrene sets in, a centre of infection begins to spread . . . . At the end of all the racial pride that has been encouraged, all the boastfulness that has been displayed, a poison has been injected into the veins of Europe and, slowly but surely, the continent proceeds towards *savagery*.

. . . It would be worthwhile to study clinically, in detail, the steps taken by Hitler and Hitlerism to reveal to the very distinguished, very humanistic, very Christian bourgeois of the twentieth century that . . . what he cannot forgive Hitler for is not *crime* in itself, the *crime against man*, it is not *the humiliation of man as such*, it is the crime against the white man, the humiliation of the white man, and the fact that he applied to Europe colonialist procedures which until then had been reserved exclusively for the Arabs of Algeria, the coolies of India and the blacks of Africa.

Source: Aimé Césaire, trans. 1972: *Discourse on colonialism*. New York: Monthly Review Press, pp. 13–14

FURTHER READING

Clayton, A. 1994. *The wars of French decolonization*. Harlow: Longman.
Concise accounts of France's colonial wars and unrepublican actions in Madagascar, Indo-China and North Africa.

Miller, C. L. 1995. Unfinished business: colonialism in Sub-Saharan Africa and the ideals of the French Revolution. In Klaits, J. and Haltzel, M. (eds) *The global ramifications of the French Revolution*. Cambridge: Cambridge University Press, pp. 105–25.
Brief examination of the incompatibility of imperial rule and the founding values of the French Republic.

Mortimer, E. 1969. *France and the Africans 1944–1960*. London: Faber and Faber.
Readable introduction to the background and consequences of the Brazzaville Conference.

8

May 1968: workers against the Republic?

Nick Parsons

INTRODUCTION

In May and June 1968, the largest strike wave in French history hit the country when workers joined students in protests against the Gaullist government. Consensus around the ten-year-old Fifth Republic appeared fragile as workers and students took to the streets in what many feared was another revolutionary moment in French history. And yet, President **Charles de Gaulle** managed to defuse the situation merely by calling for fresh parliamentary elections. He even managed to ensure that his party, under the leadership of **Maurice Couve de Murville**, won these elections. So, to what extent did May 1968 pose a threat to the Republic? While not under-estimating the importance of the student movement in May 1968, this chapter will concentrate on the relationship between the working class and the Republic to answer this question. This is because the working class, those people that need to sell their labour in order to survive, have, in theory, the most to gain from the central Republican value of equality. However, they have often had to engage in bitter and bloody struggles to win favourable reform, despite the fact that the outcome of such reform has often fallen far short of their hopes for equality, particularly in the economic sphere. Indeed, the integration of workers into the Republic has a long and often problematic history in France.

WORKERS AND THE REPUBLIC: A HISTORY

Throughout the nineteenth century, worker uprisings were brutally repressed in the name of economic liberalism and property rights. The doctrine of economic liberalism asserted that economic regulation should be left to the market and its laws of supply and demand as the best means of ensuring the creation and just distribution of wealth. Employment was therefore considered to be based on an individual contract and collective organizations of workers were outlawed as a threat that would push up wages artificially. The problem here was that workers needed work just to survive and were in competition with each other for employment. In short, they could never hope to improve their condition unless they acted collectively. The bourgeoisie, controlling the means of production (the land, materials and capital), could easily dominate workers and impose low wages while workers competed for jobs. Furthermore, worker aspirations for social and economic equality, in addition to political equality and equality before the law, were considered to be threats to the whole social order and the property rights upon which the power of the bourgeoisie was based.

With the creation of the Third Republic in 1870, many workers saw the new regime as offering the chance for the social and economic reforms they desired. However, glaring economic and social inequalities continued due to the slow pace and weak impact of reforms, while draconian discipline in the workplace was backed up by the State's brutal handling of worker protest, including the shooting of strikers on occasion. Nevertheless, the integration of workers into the Republic seemed to be confirmed in 1914. In that year, French workers obeyed the call to arms and went off to fight for the nation in spite of attempts by the main trade union organization, the *Confédération Générale du Travail* (General Confederation of Labour, CGT), to organize a general strike against the war.

Such integration, however, was partial at best. The workers' movement was split between reformists and revolutionaries. The former saw the Republican framework as one within which reform could be won through struggle. The latter argued that reform was pointless and a complete change of the political, economic and social order was needed for any meaningful improvement in the workers' conditions. When the Popular Front government was elected in 1936, workers thought their time had come. For the first time ever, the Socialist Party, then called the *Section Française de l'Internationale Ouvrière* (French Section of the Workers' International, SFIO) was participating in a government that was also supported by the *Parti Communiste Français* (French Communist Party, PCF). A wave of strikes followed resulting in considerable gains for workers: a 40-hour week, increased wages, workplace representation in the form of worker delegates and, for the first time, paid holidays (two weeks). These gains, however, were quickly clawed back by employers who presented them as unpatriotic in the build-up to the Second World War. The revenge of employers was complete with the banning of trade unions and of the PCF under the wartime Vichy regime.

After the Second World War, the actions of Communists in the Resistance and the profiteering and collaboration of employers gave the Left the upper hand. The PCF emerged as the largest party and formed part of the governing coalitions of 1944–1947 with the Socialists and the Christian Democrats. The CGT and other trade unions were also legitimized as patriotic organizations and were given rights to bargain collectively on behalf of all French workers. By a law of 1945, all companies employing more than 50 workers were obliged to institute works committees to enable employee views to be heard. At the national level, trade unions, along with employers and state officials, were given seats on the newly created Economic and Social Council which was to examine all legislation passing through parliament and give recommendations on it. Furthermore, national and regional Planning Commissions were created to oversee the running of the economy. Once again, trade unions were given seats on these, alongside employers and state officials. Economic liberalism was to give way to economic planning to ensure that all, and not just the privileged few, benefited from economic growth.

The post-war decades also witnessed the creation of a generalized welfare state offering workers protection against poverty due to old age, accident, illness and unemployment. To all intents and purposes, after long years of struggle, the Fourth Republic (which became the Fifth Republic in 1958) had finally succeeded in offering workers what they had long been seeking. Improved rights of political representation and improved economic and social conditions promised to reinforce the political and legal rights French workers had conquered during the previous century. So why did workers so readily support the students in May 1968? The following sections will first outline the events of May–June 1968, before examining worker motivations.

THE EVENTS OF MAY 1968

Workers did not join the strike wave of May 1968 until the middle of the month but, when they did, it gave the 'events' their potentially revolutionary character. The origins of the events lay in a growing student protest movement. The general background was provided by the Vietnam War and the growth in student numbers throughout the 1960s that had led to overcrowding in French universities. The governing structures of French universities were also challenged, especially at the campus at Nanterre in Paris that was to provide the focus for initial student discontent. Despite the existence of a university council on which student representatives sat, these provided for little student input. Indeed, university life was, by and large, dictated by rigid authoritarian structures that were out of touch with the young students who had come to fill the expanding institutions. Not only were courses seen as uninspiring and designed to reproduce social elites but a strict social control also operated. Indeed, the question of sexual freedom had already seen verbal clashes between students and university authorities as segregation in university residences offered little independence to students.

Student demonstrations and strikes had already taken place in the month leading up to the events considered to be the immediate cause of May 1968. In mid-March, violent demonstrations took place in Paris against the

American campaign in Vietnam and several students were arrested. On 22 March at Nanterre, a meeting to protest against these arrests led to the occupation of the administrative building in the campus by what became known as the *Mouvement du 22 Mars* (Movement of the 22 March), or the M22M, under the leadership of **Daniel Cohn-Bendit**, a second-year sociology student. In response, the university was closed and eight members of the M22M ordered to appear before a disciplinary committee at the Sorbonne on 6 May.

On 3 May, protests against these actions took place at the Sorbonne. When police entered the university and herded 500 students into vans, violent clashes broke out. These continued in the following days, culminating in a police attempt to clear the Latin Quarter of barricades erected by the students. Students hurling paving stones and Molotov cocktails were met by indiscriminate police attacks that caused innocent bystanders, as well as rioting students, to be injured. As the police faced universal condemnation, the CGT, the *Confédération Française Démocratique du Travail* (the Democratic French Confederation of Labour, CFDT), and the *Fédération de l'Education Nationale* (the National Education Federation) called for a 24-hour general strike to protest at police brutality. This resulted in mass demonstrations in Paris and many other cities. Yet, even before it took place, on 11 May, Prime Minister **Georges Pompidou** announced that student demands would be met.

Despite this, students continued their protest movement, occupying the Sorbonne when the government gave in to pressure and reopened it. While they established a 'student commune' in which debates questioned all aspects of contemporary society, the focus of discontent switched to workers. Among these, it was particularly younger workers who went on strike and occupied factories the length and breadth of France in the weeks that followed. Estimates of the numbers out on strike at the height of the movement, around 23 and 24 May, vary between seven and 11 million out of a total workforce of some 14 million. What is not in doubt, however, is that in total some 150,000,000 working days were lost in 1968, the overwhelming majority of them in the two months of May and June, resulting in total economic and political paralysis.

The impression of a total collapse of state authority was reinforced when workers in mass meetings everywhere followed the lead given by Renault workers at Boulogne-Billancourt and rejected a deal hammered out between representatives of the State, employers and trade unions (who did not sign it but agreed to present it to the strikers for approval) between 25 and 27 May. The deal, known as the Grenelle Agreement, made considerable concessions to the workers. Wages were to rise by 10 per cent across the board, with minimum wages to rise by 35 per cent; the working week was to return to 40 hours after having risen due to economic expansion and restructuring; and trade unions were to be given the right to establish workplace branches for the first time in history. Despite what were major concessions from employers, the leader of the CGT, **Georges Séguy,** had no option but to back a continuation of the strike when the meeting of 10,000 Renault workers rejected the deal, calling for 'a government of the people'.

The non-Communist Left appeared to be organizing itself, ready to step into what was looking like a power vacuum. At a mass rally in the Charléty Stadium on 27 May, the CGT was criticized as betraying the socialist cause due to its attempt to negotiate a settlement to the conflict. The following day, **François Mitterrand,** the head of the *Fédération de la Gauche Démocratique et Socialiste* (Federation of the Democratic and Socialist Left), proposed that **Pierre Mendès France,** a member of the *Parti Socialiste Unifié* (United Socialist Party, PSU) should form a provisional government if Pompidou's government were to fall. These events were overshadowed on 29 May, however, by the news that the President of the Republic, Charles de Gaulle, had disappeared. On the pretext of spending time at his home in Colombey-les-Deux-Églises, he in fact went to Baden-Baden in Germany where he met General **Massu,** the commander of French forces there, to ensure that he had the support of the military should it be required.

On his return to Paris on 30 May, de Gaulle announced that there would be fresh parliamentary elections. This manoeuvre was sufficient to divide the protesters and defuse the situation. While the PSU and *Union Nationale des Étudiants de France* (National Union of French Students), protested against de Gaulle's policy, arguing that elections represented a 'bourgeois trap', the CGT turned its attention towards them. Workers began to drift back to work, although a few remained on strike until July. A scared public opinion turned against the students as elections were seen as permitting the democratic expression of opinion. All demonstrations were banned until the elections and the Sorbonne and Odéon Theatre, which had also been occupied by students, were cleared in mid-June.

On 23 June 1968, in the first round of the elections, the Gaullists, campaigning as the *Union pour la Défense de la République* (Union for the Defence of the Republic), and their allies gained an impressive 46 per cent of the vote. After the second round, a week later, they had won an overwhelming majority, with 358 seats out of 485. What had appeared to be another revolutionary moment in French history had ended, not with a bang but with a whimper, as a shaken electorate, including one in four workers, voted for law and order and stability. So, was this really a revolutionary threat to the Republic from disaffected workers? Or are there other explanations for the attitudes of the strikers during the heady days of May 1968?

May 1968 in Peugeot–Sochaux

The Peugeot car assembly plant in Sochaux was one of the largest and most modern in France at the time, employing 25,000 workers, and the strike which broke out there shows some characteristic traits of the strikes of May 1968.

In the first half of the 1960s, frequent strikes had occurred over pay, work rates and assembly-line work. Apart from a strike for a fourth week's holiday in 1963, these had ended in failure. Management repression, including the sacking of trade union officials, had led to poor workplace relations and a workforce lacking in confidence about the possibility of change. Carried along by national events, however, the unions presented new demands to the management and voted to go on strike and occupy the factory on 20 May. Only a minority of workers, fluctuating between 100 and 1,000, occupied the factory. Most merely stayed away.

Management and unions at Sochaux waited for the lead to be given by events at the national level before taking any action. Thus, the unions only asked for negotiations on 28 May, following the Grenelle Agreement, while the management only agreed to talks on 31 May, following de Gaulle's announcement of parliamentary elections. A return to work was agreed for 10 June. However, the strike immediately broke out again on the initiative of some activists. The next day, the management called in the police to clear the occupied factory, resulting in violent confrontations during which two workers were killed. The factory was cleared and closed pending agreement to end the conflict. This was reached on 20 June, with the elections approaching and the strike running out of steam. The next day, after 31 days, the strike ended, with workers gaining a 12 per cent pay rise, a reduction to the 46-hour working week and new trade union rights from a hitherto intransigent management.

MAY 1968 AND WORKER DEMANDS

May 1968 occurred as a result of a series of complex crises coming together at the same point in time. The fuse was lit by the crisis in higher education. A further generational aspect to the events was that most demonstrators were young. They were rebelling against the hierarchical nature of French society, with its moralistic overtones, in the context of a nascent 'youth culture'. Consumer society was also a target, blamed for crushing the spiritual needs of the people under the weight of rampant materialism. Workers initially joined the movement in protest at the heavy-handed manner with which the police dealt with the student demonstrators. Their entry onto the scene generalized the political nature of the crisis by bringing the country to a standstill and giving it the appearance of a classic class conflict in which workers rose up to overthrow their bourgeois oppressors.

But is this last interpretation really true? Some extreme left-wing elements, particularly in the student movement but also among the working classes, certainly saw the events of May 1968 as a possible revolution. However, such an interpretation sits uneasily with the supposed integration of workers into the Republic at the end of the Second World War. While the other social, political and cultural aspects of May 1968 are not insignificant, this section will examine the primary concerns of workers in order to ascertain what such views said about the relationship between the workers and the Republic at this time.

First, most of the workers' concerns were the traditional ones of job security and wages (see Extract 8.1). The French economy had experienced a long and sustained boom since the end of the Second World War and had been thoroughly modernized. The pace of modernization accelerated from 1958 onwards as the State encouraged industrial concentration through company mergers, creating larger companies capable of competing in emerging world markets. For many years, the spectre of unemployment seemed to be consigned to the dustbin of history, kept alive only in the memories of those who had experienced the depression of the 1930s. From the mid-1960s, however, it raised its ugly head again. By 1967, unemployment had risen to nearly 400,000. This was a psychological shock to generations that had assumed full employment and increasing living standards were here to stay. In addition, economic modernization was based on increasing production through the application of assembly-line technology. This required an unskilled workforce that would merely perform simple repetitive tasks at a pace set by the machinery it operated. As a result, although wages were higher for the millions who had moved from agriculture to industrial labour in the decades after the war, they were still low, especially for the mass of unskilled factory workers. Whereas middle-class students could rail against the spiritual ravages of the consumer society, workers wanted a greater opportunity to taste the pleasures it afforded.

What marked May 1968 out as different from previous strike movements, however, was the emergence of new demands from workers. These were concerned with the quality of working life and most forcefully expressed by the CFDT. The events of May 1968 radicalized the union and it began to advocate *autogestion* (workers' self-management). This argued for the nationalization (state ownership) of industry but advocated that workplaces should be run by managers elected by the workforce. Through their trade unions, workers would participate in national economic management via a system of democratic planning. Local workplace union branches would participate in local economic plans that would feed into regional, then national plans. In this manner, a decentralized planning structure would ensure that workers would have a say in national economic management, ensuring a 'bottom-up' planning process in contrast to the traditional top-down structure. Such ideas gained widespread appeal in the ideologically charged days of May 1968.

The emergence and appeal of *autogestion* say much about the manner in which French workers had been integrated into French Republican structures over the previous 20 years. French economic growth in the post-war period was based upon the implementation of assembly-line production processes that left workers with little or no discretion over how to do their jobs. In other words, the control of production processes was firmly in the hands of the managers and engineers who designed and oversaw production. In addition, French employers were notoriously anti-trade union, particularly in the small and medium-sized companies that predominated in France. Although they had accepted employee delegates after the 1936 Popular Front strike wave and works committees after the Liberation, many French employers simply ignored the law. Where they did exist, these channels of employee representation were seen as a lesser evil than the admittance of trade unions into the workplace. Even though, in reality, trade union candidates dominated them, they were elected by the whole workforce and were therefore not trade union bodies. In effect, they enabled some form of employee representation while excluding trade unions from the workplace. Furthermore, their decision-making rights were strictly limited and in most cases works committees were reduced to playing a social role in the workplace, such as running the works canteen or organizing holiday camps for the children of workers. Thus, any collective voice for workers was largely silenced by the legal exclusion of trade unions from the workplace.

The representatives of labour were also excluded from national economic management. First, the tripartite Economic and Social Council and Planning Commissions gave the chance of some input into policy-making but this input was minor due to the dominance of state technocrats and politicians. Indeed, the CGT left the bodies in 1947 not to return until the 1980s in protest at the poor influence they wielded. The political representatives of the working class too were excluded from power. The majority of workers voted for the PCF in the years up to 1968 and, even in the elections of that year, nearly half still did so. However, after it was forced out of government in the Cold War climate of 1947, the workers' movement was deprived of any effective political channel. The advent of a more centralized state, with the founding of the Fifth Republic in 1958, ensured that the PCF remained an opposition party until 1981 when it formed a very junior partner in President **François Mitterrand**'s Socialist–Communist coalition.

Workers thus lacked solid trade union defences in the workplace and employers refused to negotiate with them. They also lacked effective political defences in parliament and in the bodies that fed into the political decision-making process. In effect, the working classes' integration into the French Republic's political and economic structures was based upon their acceptance of a subordinate role in the workplace and in the wider society. Management ruled the workplace, while political government was focused upon the promotion of business interests, particularly from 1958 onwards, in an attempt to forge a modern economy. Integration was to take place on an individual level through increased standards of living, while workers collectively were excluded from the exercise of any political or economic power or influence. The result was that sustained economic growth was secured at the expense of any worker control over working life or the direction of society. The only manner in which they could effectively make their voices heard was through periodic industrial unrest. Trade unions, lacking any foothold in the workplace, naturally channelled such protest to the national level and directed it against the State in the hope of securing legislative reform.

Such exclusion from power was accepted by the generations that moved from agriculture to industry in the post-war years as it at least offered them improved living standards. Their discontent was mainly shown in voting for Communist candidates and through sporadic industrial militancy which at least offered a means of securing wage gains. With the entry into the labour market of the generations born after the war, however, things changed. They had higher aspirations and were better educated than their parents. They were no longer prepared to accept the rigid hierarchy of the workplace and their own subordinate position within that hierarchy. Nor were they prepared to accept the exhausting, boring and dehumanizing work offered by assembly-line production processes. Hence, young workers were in the forefront of the strike movement and their demands for *autogestion* reflected wider social demands for a freer, less constraining and more democratic society.

While some workers may have hoped, or even believed, that the time for revolution had come, it is doubtful that this was the aspiration of the majority. Workers' demands suggest that, while economic growth may have gone some way to improving standards of living, the desire for autonomy at work and participation in decision-making processes had been overlooked. In this respect, demands for *autogestion* should be seen as a response to tight managerial control of the workplace and excessive state centralization. Strikers challenged the Gaullist version of a centralized, technocratic state in which everything was sacrificed on the altar of economic modernization rather than the Republic *per se*. Having won their equality before the law and the right to vote, workers were now demanding an extension of the notion of democracy to include influence in economic and industrial spheres. In a paradoxical manner, workers engaged in strike action that was given a quasi-revolutionary hue by its juxtaposition with the more ideologically informed students' movement. Unlike the students, however, French workers did not intend to overthrow Republican institutions but to secure a greater integration into them through their democratization.

CONCLUSIONS: TOWARDS INDUSTRIAL DEMOCRACY?

As far as workers are concerned, the immediate consequence of the end of the strike movement was that the previously rejected Grenelle Agreement became the basis for collective bargaining. Wages were raised in line with the agreement, representing a considerable improvement for the lowest paid members of the workforce. However, such gains were subsequently eroded by an 11 per cent devaluation of the franc in August 1969 and by inflation as employers pushed the costs onto consumers. More importantly in the longer term, legislation was passed in December 1968 giving trade unions the right to set up workplace branches in companies employing 50 or more people. Some 84 years after gaining legal recognition, trade unions had finally breached the employer's citadel. In theory, they now could organize workers collectively free from harassment in the workplace.

Indeed, in the wake of the crippling economic effect of the May 1968 strike wave, the government sought to shore up the position of trade unions. Political division among trade unions and anti-union employer practices ensured that they were traditionally very weak in France with a high point of only one in four wage-earners unionized in the immediate post-war period. This fell to one in five in 1968. What had become apparent was that economic change could not be handled smoothly in France because of the weakness of union organizations and their consequent inability to function as intermediary bodies between workers, employers and the State. In France, the State had traditionally been suspicious of intermediary organizations with the peak governing structures of the nation – the President and parliament – considered to be the ultimate expression of the will of the people. In addition to this, the consultation of such intermediary bodies has generally been a low priority for policy-makers. The problem with this was that worker frustrations, both within the workplace and within the wider society, could find no outlet and no solution until they boiled over into a social explosion.

In the aftermath of May 1968, it was realized that continued economic modernization required social reform to channel discontent and avoid costly disruption in increasingly capital-intensive and interdependent industries. The most important consequence of May 1968 for workers may, therefore, be found in government attempts to provide structures through which worker demands could be discussed. In 1971, new legislation endorsed company-level collective agreements in an attempt to decentralize industrial relations and to defuse potential conflicts at the lowest level possible. Real reform, however, had to wait until 1982 and a package of legislation known as the Auroux Laws. These made annual company-level collective bargaining over wages

compulsory in all companies employing 50 or more people. Furthermore, in a measure proposed by the CFDT, workers were given the right to express their views on work in 'self-expression groups' which had to meet during working time. This measure was presented by the then Minister of Labour, **Jean Auroux**, as giving workers 'citizenship' within the company.

The impact of the laws fell far short of their ambitions, and yet employers have had to become far more aware and considerate of the needs of their employees in the workplace and now use a range of mechanisms to consult with them. While employers undoubtedly learnt some harsh lessons in May 1968, evolving economic circumstances may be of far more importance in explaining this change of attitude. More intense global economic competition, and an increased emphasis on quality and innovation in production, require far greater cooperation and active participation in problem-solving from workforces than previously. On the other hand, French workers have, in their vast majority, accepted the realities of capitalism. Again, this may be due to the shock they experienced when faced with the possibility of radical social change in 1968. However, changing political contexts may be more significant in explaining worker attitudes. The break-up of Soviet Russia deprived the Communist Left of its model of reference, while the failure of President Mitterrand to find a socialist solution to the economic crisis in 1981–82 led many to the conclusion that 'you can't buck the market'.

This is not to say that May 1968 has faded into irrelevancy for workers. Student demonstrators in 1986 were heard to shout '68 c'est vieux, 86 c'est mieux' (68 is old, 86 is better). Rather, what May 1968 brought home was the need to integrate workers fully into the fabric of French capitalist and Republican structures. Changing attitudes in the workplace and in wider society suggest that the message was at least heard. Continuing widespread authoritarian management, including anti-unionism, and increasing social inequalities suggest, however, that there is still some way to go before the central Republican values of democracy and equality can be said to have fully filtered down to those whose only economic asset is the labour they can sell. Indeed, the decentralization of industrial relations since the Auroux Laws has increased flexibility in the workplace, including the hiring and firing of workers and the use of part-time and temporary labour. High levels of unemployment in the 1980s and 1990s have also excluded many from the fruits of economic modernization and growth. The State is still attempting to grapple with such problems.

In 1998 and 2000, legislation was passed to reduce the working week to 35 hours. This aimed to mobilize Republican notions of equality and solidarity and to introduce 'job-sharing' on a national level in order to soak up unemployment. However, these reforms provoked virulent employer opposition who argued that such reforms were counter to entrepreneurial freedom and threatened French industrial competitiveness. Such views suggest that the economic antagonisms associated with capitalist society continue to represent a major obstacle to any consensus over French Republican values. The integration of French workers into key economic, social and political institutions still has some way to go.

Extract 8.1: Les Militants Syndicalistes CGT, CFDT, FEN, du *Mouvement Révolutionnaire*, Paris, 11 June 1968

NOUS REPRENDRONS LE COMBAT JUSQU'A LA VICTOIRE

Pendant quinze jours ou trois semaines, nous avons été près de 10 millions en grève. Nos revendications étaient les mêmes. Tout le monde s'accorde à dire que notre mouvement a été le plus puissant jamais vu en France, plus puissant même qu'en 1936 . . . . Et pourtant nous n'avons obtenu que des miettes de ce que nous voulons.

Nous avons obtenus . . .

– des *augmentations*, les plus souvent *hiérarchisées* – qui donnent 10 000 F aux directeurs à chaque fois qu'on en a touché 1 000 à la base et qui seront dévorées demain par la hausse des prix et l'inflation.

– des *diminutions d'horaires dérisoires* que les patrons rattrapent en accélérant les cadences – et qui n'augmentent pas sensiblement nos loisirs – et ne règlent en rien le *chômage de 700 000 jeunes*, prévu par le Ve plan.

– des *acomptes* sur les journées de grève le plus souvent *à récupérer* – . . .

Nous voulons . . .

– des *augmentations égales pour tous* qui réduisent progressivement la hiérarchie jusqu'à un maximum de 1 à 4

– *l'échelle mobile des salaries* qui rétablit automatiquement le pouvoir d'achat à chaque hausse des prix ou dévaluation de la monnaie

– les *40 heures tout de suite* . . . sans diminution de salaire et si cela ne suffit pas à donner du travail à tous

– *l'échelle mobile des heures de travail*, pour répartir le travail disponible entre les bras et les cerveaux disponibles –

– le *paiement intégral* et sans condition *des journées de grève* dont la prolongation incombe au patronat qui refuse nos justes revendications

– *l'exercice libre du syndicalisme* dans l'entreprise qui permette à tous les travailleurs à s'organiser.

WE WILL CARRY ON THE STRUGGLE UNTIL WE SECURE VICTORY

For two to three weeks, almost 10 million of us have been on strike. Our demands have been the same. Everyone agrees that our movement is the

most powerful ever seen in France, more powerful even than in 1936
. . . . And yet we have only won a tiny amount of what we want.

We have won . . .
– wage rises, more often than not differentiated – which give 10,000 FF
to managers every time that those at the bottom are given only 1,000 FF,
an amount which will be eaten up tomorrow by price rises and inflation.
– derisory reductions in the working week that bosses claw back by
speeding up work rates – and which do not add in any significant way to
our leisure time.
– and do nothing to reduce youth unemployment, forecast to rise to
700,000 by the 5th Plan
– payment for strike days, the lost production of which will often have to
be made up
– . . .

We want . . .
– equal pay rises for all that progressively reduce wage differentials until
they reach a maximum of 1 to 4
– a flexible salary scale that automatically safeguards buying power after
each price rise or devaluation of the franc
– the immediate introduction of a 40-hour week . . . without a pay cut
and if this is not enough to give everyone work
– flexible working hours so that the work available can be shared
between the brain and brawn of those able to work
– full and unconditional payment for days lost due to the strike, the
continuation of which is the responsibility of the bosses and managers
who refuse our fair demands
– the free exercise of trade unionism in the workplace, allowing all
workers to organize themselves collectively.

FURTHER READING

Capdevielle, J. and Mouriaux, R. 1988. *Mai 68: l'entre-deux de la modernité –
histoire de trente ans*. Paris: Presses de la FNSP.
Examines the events of May 1968 by placing them in their long-term social,
economic and political context.
Hanley, D. L. and Kerr, A. P. 1989. *May 68: coming of age*. London:
Macmillan.
An edited collection covering the educational, political and cultural aspects
of May 1968.
Reader, K. A. with Wadia, K. 1993. *The May 1968 events in France:
reproductions and Interpretations*. London: St Martin's Press.
A wide-ranging overview of different interpretations of the events and of
their representation.

9

The campaign for parity in the 1990s: women and the French Republic

Hanna Diamond and Claire Gorrara

INTRODUCTION

On 28 June 1999 at a specially convened Congress in Versailles, the Senate and the National Assembly ratified a government bill that revised Articles three and four of the French Constitution of 1958. Article three was amended to read that 'la loi favorise l'égal accès des femmes et des hommes aux mandats électoraux et fonctions électives' (the law favours the equal access of men and women to political office). Article four made it incumbent on political parties that they 'contribuent à la mise en œuvre de la parité' (contribute to the implementation of parity). These revisions of the French Constitution enshrined in law the principle of parity or numerical equality for women and men in terms of political representation. This decision was heralded as a great victory for women. Pro-parity campaigners declared that it gave women their first real opportunity to play a full part in the French political process, thereby promising to change the very nature of democratic life under the Fifth Republic.

This chapter will set the campaign for parity within a French historical perspective, before focusing on the events of the late 1990s that led up to this momentous decision. It will then address some of the central issues that opposed pro- and anti-parity campaigners, such as the debates over gender equality and difference, competing models of political representation and the notion of women's citizenship. The chapter will conclude with an assessment of the elections in March 2001, where parity was applied as part of the electoral process for the first time.

FRENCH WOMEN AND POLITICAL REPRESENTATION

The history of French women's participation in Republican political life is one of exclusion. During the French Revolution, women's political activity was relegated to the margins and women were kept out of mainstream politics. For successive Republican regimes during the nineteenth century, the refusal to allow women political rights was also grounded in more immediate reasons of political expediency. Fearing the effects of a much expanded electorate and the potential for divisive civil war, they curbed the number of those eligible to vote or to be leaders with restrictions based upon sex, property, ownership and age. Throughout the nineteenth century, women continued to remain outside a body politic that came to be identified with a standard, abstract (hu)man subject on whom Republican principles of universalism would be based.

Legal and ideological obstacles to women gaining access to politics were, however, contested by a growing women's suffrage movement in France in the late nineteenth and early twentieth centuries. Campaigners and supporters of votes for women repeatedly came up against resistance on the part of the Republican establishment when it came to the granting of political rights. In 1919, the Chamber of Deputies passed draft legislation giving women full political rights for the first time, but the Senate (or upper house) blocked it in 1922. This process was repeated a number of times during the inter-war period as the stalemate continued. Conservative opposition to women's suffrage was often swelled by Centre–Left politicians, who feared that women were 'naturally' more conservative and religious than men, and would therefore support the political Right and the power of the clergy. However, women did enter government during this period as members of a short-lived Popular Front administration (1936–37), when three women were nominated to ministerial posts. On the eve of the Second World War, when many other nations had granted women political rights, French women were still denied a political voice.

During the Second World War and the Occupation of France by German forces, the pro-collaborationist Vichy regime demonstrated its hostility to any progressive social or political agenda for women. Its motto, *famille, travail, patrie* (family, work, homeland), illustrated its attitude to women as primarily home-makers and reproductive machines who would fulfil their natural role by repeopling a depleted France. With the victory of the Allies and France's resistance forces in 1944, a new spirit of cooperation and hope promised change and, in 1944, women were granted the right to vote. In the first legislative elections held under universal suffrage, 5.7 per cent of the elected deputies in the Lower House were women. A number of them had been active in the French Resistance and had some experience of political activism.

Throughout the 1950s and 1960s, women's groups continued to campaign on issues close to women's lives and concerns, such as the right to contraception and the decriminalization of abortion. However, over these decades, the numbers of women elected to the National Assembly dropped steadily. During the early years of the Fifth Republic, the percentage of women representatives in the National Assembly remained static at between 1.5 and 2 per cent, far below the levels of the late 1940s. It seemed that rates of women's political participation were regressing. Commentators debated why there were so few women deputies. For much of the 1960s, women trusted to political education, natural evolution and the virtues of time, which, they were told, would enable them to engage in a full range of political activities.

The events of May 1968 appeared to usher in an era of change and transformation as new forms of left-wing politics challenged the established social order and the power of France's post-war political elites. One of the major legacies of this period was the French women's liberation movement, which was modelled to some extent on its American sister. It raised the profile of issues to do with women's civil and legal rights, education, employment, women's control of their bodies and sexuality and, more tangentially, political representation. Yet, for some feminist activists in the 1970s, increasing women's political representation was a 'reformist' move that clashed with their aim to overturn the whole political system. To be involved in mainstream politics was seen by these feminists as a betrayal of their cause. For such revolutionary feminists, the Republican political order had been devised and evolved without women and they could not be merely inserted into its masculine political structures. More radical policies and actions were required that challenged established hierarchies from outside the political mainstream.

By the early 1980s, the more radical currents in the French women's movement had lost ground. However, feminist activists who believed in the importance of changing the political system from within continued to militate for legal reform and equality between men and women. With the election of **François Mitterrand** as French President in 1981, the Ministry of Women's Rights was created, headed by **Yvette Roudy**. It seemed that women's rights would be at the forefront of the political agenda. This high status for state-sponsored feminism – the establishment of a specific Ministry – came in the wake of the Secretariat for the Status of Women set up by the previous conservative administration and it promised much. But, although the Ministry had ambitious projects, particularly in the areas of work and training, the final text of laws such as the 1983 *loi Roudy* on equality at work were disappointing. By the late 1980s, therefore, the equality so eagerly awaited by women had failed to materialize and many women had lost faith and patience with established systems. Attention turned to the party political culture and the nature of the political system, regarded by some as responsible for perpetuating the dominance of men in politics. For some feminist activists had come round to the idea that the only way forward was to embark upon a campaign that would garner collective support and increase the representation of women and women's concerns in the French political arena.

THE CAMPAIGN FOR PARITY IN THE 1990s

By the beginning of the 1990s, French women's participation in the political process appeared to have progressed little since the late 1940s. In 1993, 6 per cent of French deputies were women, a rise of 0.3 per cent from 1945, the year of the first legislative elections in which women could vote and stand as candidates. In comparison to France's European neighbours, this figure placed France among the bottom seven nations in which women accounted for 10 per cent or fewer of elected national representatives. Parity campaigners pointed to the success of Finland, Denmark, Norway and Sweden in including women in the political mainstream: in these countries over 30 per cent of the representatives in the lower or single chamber were women, and this had been achieved through a system of quotas. And so, the major focus of French attempts to increase the political representation of women was to be the call for constitutional reform. This inevitably set pro-parity campaigners in conflict with the universalist principles at the heart of the Republican model of democracy and enshrined in the 1958 Constitution. For the Constitution decreed that all citizens should be treated equally regardless of race, sex, creed or any other distinction. The parity campaign would come to challenge the interpretation and implementation of such political ideals.

Calls for numerical equality for men and women in political office had already been a feature of international, European, and French political debate in the decades preceding the parity campaign of the 1990s. In 1979, at a United Nations conference on ending sex discrimination, member countries were invited to include the principle of equality between men and women in their Constitutions. In France this had in fact been in place for many years: the preamble to the 1946 French Constitution set out this principle and it was repeated in the 1958 Constitution. But the UN conference also suggested implementing quotas, to which the French political climate was far more hostile. In 1982, feminist lawyer Gisèle Halimi proposed draft legislation introducing quotas for municipal elections. This bill was overturned by the French Constitutional Council which ruled that all citizens were equally eligible for political office and that quotas would unfairly favour women candidates.

During the late 1980s and early 1990s, a number of left-wing and more marginal political parties in France attempted to institute selection processes that promoted women candidates, particularly in elections taking place under proportional representation. At the same time, European directives and initiatives were moving towards the notion of a *démocratie paritaire* (democracy based on parity). In 1992, two prominent French women politicians, **Édith Cresson** and **Simone Veil**, signed an accord in Rome pledging to work for the greater participation of women in political life. 1992 was also a watershed year because *Au Pouvoir, Citoyennes! Liberté, Égalité, Parité* (Female Citizens, Take Power! Liberty, Equality, Parity) was published. This text was to become a rallying cry for a concerted campaign to increase women's political representation. From the debate and controversy provoked by this book came the founding of a number of organizations bringing together impressive numbers of women, organizations such as *Parité* (Parity) and *Elles Aussi* (Her Too). These groups worked in coordination with a network of other pressure groups to advance the cause of parity. Their actions were reported in the news-sheet, *Parité-Infos* (Parity Information). French feminists were remarkably united and mobilized in this campaign for parity, more so than they had been for over a decade.

As momentum for a change within France increased, so political parties and key political players began to take account more fully of the strength of popular support for parity. In 1994, six *listes paritaires* (candidate lists based on parity) were presented for the European elections by political parties such as the Greens and the French Socialist Party. They contained equal numbers of men and women, placed alternately. In the same year, several bills were presented to the National Assembly advocating either parity or a series of measures to ensure the greater equality of men and women in political office. By the time of the presidential elections of 1995, almost all the parties and candidates were aware of the importance of showing their support for parity. And, in the aftermath of the elections, President **Jacques Chirac** created the *Observatoire de la Parité* (Parity Observatory) to report back on the representation of women in all areas of public life, including politics, and to suggest measures to improve the current situation.

Pressure increased on the conservative government to tackle the issue of parity in the run-up to legislative elections in September 1997. Ten senior women politicians published a 'manifesto for parity' in the weekly current affairs magazine, *L'Express*. This brought parity to the forefront of the political agenda (see Extract 9.1). The manifesto lamented the highly masculine political culture of the day and characterized an outmoded political elite as a 'concentration of virile qualities'. The ten women signatories looked towards the increased participation of women in politics as a means of bringing France into the twenty-first century and 'feminizing the Republic'. To achieve this, they proposed a number of measures. These included the use of quotas; limiting the number of posts an individual politician could occupy simultaneously; linking party funding to efforts to support for parity; ensuring that state appointments, such as ambassadors, were equally shared between men and women; and finally, if needed, modifying the Constitution by means of a referendum.

The 1997 legislative elections witnessed almost the doubling of the percentage of women in the National Assembly, as the numbers of women deputies rose to 10.94 per cent of the total. Media interest in the issue of parity had certainly made it a hot topic, but much of the credit for the rise in women deputies was due to the increased number of women candidates presented by the victorious French Socialist Party: 17 per cent of its successful candidates were women. Subsequent regional elections in the spring of 1998 were to confirm this dramatic trend upwards, in this instance aided also by the electoral mechanisms of proportional representation.

With the 'cohabitation' of a conservative President, Jacques Chirac, and a Socialist Prime Minister, **Lionel Jospin**, after the legislative elections, the issue of parity preoccupied the minds of the most influential decision-makers in France. Both Chirac and Jospin angled to capitalize on the popularity of parity, whether from conviction or electoral expediency. In June 1998, the President and Prime Minister agreed on a text modifying the 1958 Constitution. This was subsequently amended by the Council of Ministers and presented to the National Assembly by the Minister of Justice, Élisabeth Guigou. This draft legislation amended Article three of the Constitution and restricted reform to elections and state appointments reading that 'the law favours the equal access of men and women to political office'. While some parity campaigners were disappointed with the use of the rather vague term *favoriser* (to favour) rather than *déterminer* (to guarantee), opinion polls showed that the vast majority of the public supported the draft amendment. The bill was passed unanimously in the National Assembly on 15 December 1998.

However, on its first reading in the Senate, the government bill was rejected and the senators proposed instead modifying Article four of the Constitution to place the onus on political parties to implement parity. Uproar followed and calls were heard for a referendum to circumvent the consent of the Senate and bring about constitutional reform. However, it was also at this time that a number of women spoke out to question the project of parity. In a manifesto published in *L'Express* on 11 February 1999, 14 well-respected women from different areas of French public life pledged their support for the principle of equality, but set out arguments against using the principle of parity and constitutional reform as the means to achieve this (see Extract 9.2).

Ultimately, the manifesto by these women opposed to parity proved to be out of step with public opinion. On 16 February 1999, the National Assembly passed the original government bill, followed, on 4 March, by the Senate, which inserted the revision of Article four on the contribution of political parties to the implementation of parity. At the Congress at Versailles on 28 June 1999, the three-fifths majority required to change the Constitution was achieved as deputies and senators passed the draft legislation by 741 votes to 42. With the principle of parity enshrined in the French Constitution, it remained to be seen how this would translate into the mechanisms of the electoral process itself and whether women's increased participation in the political arena would deliver the wholesale renewal of the Republican model that its proponents anticipated.

DEBATING PARITY AND THE REPUBLIC

All those involved in the debates surrounding parity seemed to start from the general premise that having more women representatives in elected assemblies was a desirable move. However, the crucial axis of the argument was the question whether an increase in women representatives would change women's lives and whether parity was necessarily the right way to bring about such transformations. Such debates converged on three main areas: equality and sexual difference in the political sphere, issues of representation and the notion of women's citizenship.

Universalism, equality and difference

The idea of universalism was central to discussions about parity. Universalism holds that all citizens are equal before the law, regardless of gender, race or creed. Citizens of the French Republic are thus theoretically gender-free. But supporters of parity argued that in practice this was not the case. In fact, they argued that the notions of citizenship and universalism which were frequently evoked to support a Republican status quo were used precisely to disguise the real nature of an essentially masculine Republic, founded on gender inequalities. From its very beginnings, the Jacobin heritage of the French Revolution had established the exclusion of women. The Republican political sphere was thus defined from the outset as men's business and misogynist traditions and expectations were set in place.

However, the idea of universalism was so embedded in French political culture that criticism of it provoked hostile reaction. The philosopher and cultural critic, **Élisabeth Badinter**, was particularly outspoken in this regard. She held that the introduction of parity would be in direct opposition to the principle of abstract universalism according to which all citizens are equal. The introduction of parity would establish a distinction between categories of citizens and thereby destroy the basis of Republican democracy. Equality, she claimed, was assured by the political irrelevance of difference and to attach political significance to membership of a certain community was to endanger the cohesion of the nation. If the Constitution were to be changed to include a clause defending parity, there would be nothing to prevent other social groups or 'minorities' making similar demands. Making claims for women as different would render it difficult to deny the legitimacy of other claims for representation.

In contrast, pro-parity campaigner **Sylviane Agacinski** claimed that women had sacrificed the question of difference for too long. The false universalism of the Republic and its abstract ideals of judicial equality had been a trap for feminists who were initially seduced by the idea of trying to conform to a male model. Previous male politicians had dismissed all demands by women as women and had obliged them to remain within the existing order. For Agacinski, the idea of national sovereignty now had to be reviewed to recognize rather than suppress sexual difference. Parity would finally enable the nation to take full account of the sexed nature of humanity.

As can be seen, ideas related to gender equality and sexual difference were used extensively by those both for and against parity. Anti-parity activists claimed that gender should not be seen as more significant than any other factor making up our identities. For them, this insistence on difference could only be counter-productive at a time when traditional ideas about sexual difference were being abandoned. Indeed, anti-parity campaigners considered that changing the Constitution and the process of political representation would ultimately work against women's fight for equality. The campaign for parity implicitly gave credence to the view that women were incapable of making it under the same conditions as men and needed preferential treatment. For them, parity might even undermine women who managed to gain political positions via this route. They agreed that there should be more women in politics but clearly supported an 'evolutionary' rather than 'revolutionary' approach, as women gradually gained more political experience and confidence.

Many pro-parity supporters argued that parity sought to eliminate sexual difference as a major factor in an individual's identity. It might be necessary to have a preliminary stage where this difference was recognized, but this would disappear once women were better established in politics and perceived as equally capable of holding powerful positions. However, in order for this to happen, women needed to be supported in their bid to enter the political mainstream with the equal distribution of parliamentary seats between men and women. For such campaigners, parity, in its simplest terms, worked towards a more equitable situation for women and ensured that both sexes had a fair share in decision-making, rectifying a previously untenable situation. It was the responsibility of the law and the Constitution to ensure that access to power was equal for both sexes.

Representation

The notion of representation also taxed the minds of pro- and anti-parity supporters. What did it mean to represent and be represented in a democracy? Under the French Republic, sovereignty emanates from the 'people' or the 'nation' and representatives are nominated members of the population. However, parity threw up two competing ideas about who these representatives should be. According to the first interpretation, they were elected members of the population who formed part of a representative body, implementing what such a body believed to be in the best interests of the nation as a whole. In order to do so, they did not need to resemble the voters. The second interpretation countered that elected representatives should reflect the diversity of the electorate and their interests. They were not disembodied members of a national community but expressed views and opinions that could be related to specific sections of society. Parity was an attempt to force a move from the first interpretation to the second.

Anti-parity activists generally believed that promoting women candidates as women was misleading and undemocratic. For them, the political system was not designed to be organized in terms of gender. Candidates for election were chosen on the basis of the constituency they represented and their party affiliations. It would be unacceptable to ask electors to vote for the candidates on the grounds of their gender rather than party policies. Indeed, it would be damaging to sub-divide national representatives into minority groupings with different and possibly competing interests. Furthermore, as the anti-parity manifesto of February 1999 made clear, the demands for parity assumed that women were a homogenous group and that there was a kind of automatic solidarity between them (see Extract 9.2). For Badinter and others, this implied leaving aside other axes of oppression that afflicted individual women, such as race and class. For them 'women' was not an absolute category as 'all women are not equally discriminated against'.

In contrast, parity supporters argued that the lack of progress for women meant that the representative body had consistently failed to represent them adequately. Parity would enable more women to enter the political arena and thereby redefine Republican politics. Women would have more influence on the mechanisms of politics, would be be more involved in decision-making and would also push for a more egalitarian form of government. The assumption by many pro-parity campaigners had been that bringing more women into formal politics would mean that women's interests would be better represented. Some parity supporters also thought that the presence of a larger 'critical mass' of women would change the nature of mainstream politics itself (see Extract 9.1). The presence of women would influence legislation and individual women would vote for changes beneficial to the majority of women, improving the status of women in society generally. Women's issues, like abortion or sexual violence, might feature more prominently on the political agenda.

Finally, what does it mean for women to represent women? Those who argued against parity questioned the existence of a defined set of 'women's interests' and whether women would indeed be best represented by other women. What may be in one woman's interests could be meaningless or even harmful for another. There is no assurance that simply because a representative is biologically female she will represent the interests of other women. Women do not necessarily express themselves in gendered terms on every question. Although the general thrust of the anti-parity campaigners on this issue is compelling, it is also the case that failure to recognize the category of 'woman' in political terms leaves women's exclusion hidden behind a sham discourse of universalism. To argue against parity on these grounds is to ignore the fact that government policies and decisions are gendered and that women constitute a powerful corrective force even if not all women identify with such a cause all of the time.

Citizenship

Parity has been seized on as a pragmatic way of improving women's situation and has proved an effective means of rallying women to the cause of equality.

However, most feminists are aware that discrimination against women cannot be remedied by correcting a gender imbalance in the political elite. A fundamental reworking not just of democracy but of society in general is necessary if parity is really to succeed in improving women's lives. As has already been established, the construction of Republican democracy was dependent on the exclusion of women. In this context, the simple addition of a female elite cannot change a wholly gendered system. Thus, it is perhaps less mainstream politics that needs to be transformed for women than social, cultural and economic structures.

Theorists have suggested that a helpful way forward would be to rethink the whole notion of women's citizenship. By widening the terms of what it means to be a female citizen, it becomes clear that it is not just civil society which needs to change, but also domestic life. Women's citizenship is affected not only by their public participation in politics and their position in the labour market, but also by gender relations within the family. Even after the introduction of parity, unless gender relations are reworked more widely, women will never succeed in having an equal share of power. The redefinition of citizenship must therefore encompass all aspects of women's lives, including domestic responsibilities. Parity may have usefully opened up the terms of these debates, but it needs to be a starting point and not an end in itself.

CONCLUSION: TOWARDS A *DÉMOCRATIE PARITAIRE*?

The election of over 38,000 town councillors on 11 and 18 March 2001 was a test case for the application of parity. These elections represented the first opportunity to assess the impact of parity on the French electoral process and its outcomes. Communes with over 3,500 inhabitants were obliged to operate according to the principle of parity with each party putting forward lists of candidates in groups of six that had to contain equal numbers of men and women. This did not necessarily mean in alternate order and it remained the case that men were generally better placed, heading 90 per cent of lists. However, the effect of parity on the electoral outcome was quite spectacular. The percentage of women town councillors rose from 22 per cent in 1995 to 47.5 per cent in 2001. Although parties on the Right had most vehemently opposed the constitutional change of parity, women candidates from these parties were some of the direct beneficiaries of parity as the conservative vote increased.

The profile of those women entering political life for the first time in March 2001 bore out to some extent the hopes of pro-parity campaigners that a new swathe of actors were waiting to enter the political arena. Research statistics showed that the new women councillors were far less likely to have been recruited via traditional party political structures than men, interpreted by some as a sign of renewal of the democratic process. In terms of their personal and professional profile, elected women town councillors were younger than their male counterparts and half as likely to be retired or aged over 60. As with the male town councillors, around a third of them came from the private sector, but women were better represented from the teaching profession and the civil service than men. Women town councillors were five times more likely to describe themselves as 'sans profession déclarée' (no stated profession), covering a multitude of possibilities from housewife to unemployed.

Yet for all the euphoria over the great increases in the number of women councillors, these statistics hid continuing inequality in terms of decision-making. As the left-leaning French daily *Libération* termed it, 'la femme investit la mairie, mais l'homme garde les clés' (women enter the town hall but the men keep the keys). For, in subsequent elections for mayor on 25 March, women made up only 6.9 per cent of mayors. Bucking previous trends, women candidates did better in larger urban agglomerations, with the French Communist Party and the Centre–Right *Union pour la Démocratie Française* (Union for French Democracy, UDF) doing well with 9.5 per cent and 7.25 per cent of women mayors respectively, and the Greens, pioneers in parity politics, with not one single woman among its 33 mayors.

When it came to nominating women to powerful positions on council executives, women fared badly too. In a number of high-profile towns, women made up over half of the executive administration, such as in Paris under the Socialist Bernard Delanoë (18 women and 15 men) and in Strasbourg under Centre–Right mayor Fabienne Keller (9 women and 7 men). Yet in a large proportion of administrations, and even those with a woman mayor, women were very poorly represented or given traditionally women-identified portfolios such as social affairs, education, culture or the environment. The more weighty portfolios of finance and budgeting were overwhelming accorded to men. Older and more established administrations tended to be the least receptive to women candidates and some regions of France proved to be more 'feminist' than others, of note Brittany, Normandy and the Loire Valley. As the *Libération* reporter noted in their special issue on parity and the council elections 31 March–1 April 2001, 'la loi a permis de faire des progrès, pas d'accomplir des miracles' (the law has brought progress but has not produced miracles).

While it is too early to predict whether parity has triggered an irreversible feminization of French political life, the first nationwide elections under parity proved the existence of a generation of women candidates ready to enter French political life given the opportunity and encouragement. Their contribution to renewing French political life has yet to be evaluated but their presence in the political arena symbolizes changing attitudes and concerns under the French Fifth Republic as it enters the twenty-first century.

Extract 9.1: 'Le manifeste des dix pour la parité', *L'Express*, 6–12 June 1996, pp. 32–3

Pourquoi des femmes venues d'horizons divers aux engagements parfois opposés, ont-elles décidé d'unir leurs voix? Ayant en commun d'avoir eu ou d'exercer actuellement des responsabilités publiques, nous voulons, alors que se profile le prochain millénaire dans un monde incertain et une France inquiète, lancer cet appel pour l'égalité des chances et des droits entre hommes et femmes. Une égalité enfin effective, au-delà des promesses de circonstance, électorales ou non. Une égalité plus urgente que jamais, non seulement pour les femmes, mais pour notre pays, car plus qu'hier encore la participation des unes va de pair avec l'intérêt national. . . .

Cet échec de la participation des femmes à la vie et aux responsabilités publiques provient d'une tradition plongeant ses racines dans un jacobinisme désormais hors de saison. Noyau de notre culture républicaine, pas toujours démocratique, le jacobinisme a d'abord et surtout été une affaire d'hommes. . . . La relation aux autres tels qu'ils sont, la sensibilité, le concret, le souci du quotidien, étaient rejetés du champ politique. Et les femmes avec. . . .

Les fonctions de représentation et d'exécution sont accaparées par un groupe dirigeant, petit en nombre, extrêmement homogène par la formation dans les grandes écoles, et une insertion précoce dans les grands corps de l'État et les cabinets ministériels. Stable dans sa composition et peu perméable dans son accès, ce groupe dirigeant constitue une « aristocratie démocratique » sous couvert d'élite républicaine. Il est grand temps d'en finir avec ces stéréotypes et ces blocages, en féminisant la République. Le regard des femmes, leur expérience, leur culture manquent cruellement au moment de l'élaboration des lois.

Débattre, éduquer, convaincre, inciter ne suffisent plus pour modifier une situation qui perdure malgré les bonnes volontés. Pour atteindre l'égalité effective des hommes et des femmes à tous les échelons et dans tous les secteurs de la société française, il faut que la politique donne l'exemple. Et pour cela, le temps est arrivé.

Une pratique renouvelée du pouvoir et de la démocratie ne sera possible que soutenue par une volonté et une pression politique sans faille. L'objectif est d'arriver, par étapes, à la parité.

'Manifesto of the ten for parity'

Why have women from different backgrounds and with sometimes opposing political views decided to unite in protest? Sharing the fact that we have occupied or occupy currently positions of public responsibility, we want to call for equality of opportunity and equal rights for men and women as the next millennium approaches in an uncertain world and an anxious France. An equality that is finally effective, that goes beyond occasional promises and electoral pledges. An equality that is more urgent than ever, not only for women, but for our country, because, even more so than in the past, the participation of women goes hand in hand with the national interest. . . .

The failure of women to participate in public life and in positions of public responsibility comes from a tradition that is rooted in a Jacobinism that is now out of date. The core of our republican, and not always democratic, culture, Jacobinism has first and foremost been a men's affair. . . . Relations with others, emotions, material concerns, everyday worries, were rejected from the political sphere. And women with them. . . .

[. . .] Executive and legislative offices are monopolized by a numerically small ruling group, all of whose members are extremely similar due to their training in the best universities and their early recruitment into top civil and diplomatic jobs and as ministerial advisers. Unchanging in its make-up and rarely open to outsiders, this ruling group represents a 'democratic aristocracy' in the guise of a republican elite. It is high time to end these stereotypes and these obstacles by feminizing the Republic. Women's perspectives, their experience, their culture are cruelly missing when laws are being formulated.

To discuss, to educate, to convince and to provoke debate are no longer enough to change a situation that has stagnated for some time despite good intentions. In order to achieve effective equality between men and women at every level and in all areas of French society, politics must give the example. And in this instance, the time has come.

A renewed practice of power and democracy will only be possible if it is supported by unwavering political will and pressure. The main objective is, by stages, to come to parity.

Extract 9.2: 'Trois arguments contre la parité', *L'Express,* **11–16 February 1999, p. 80**

La solution proposée pour mettre fin à l'indécente absence des femmes dans la vie politique est en contradiction avec l'esprit et les principes d'une politique progressiste

1. On croit pallier une insuffisance démocratique en tournant le dos à la république universelle. L'universel est une arme contre les différences en tant qu'elles séparent et discriminent. L'histoire montre qu'on n'intègre jamais au nom de la différence mais qu'en revanche c'est toujours en son nom qu'on exclut: voyez aujourd'hui comment les sociétés en voie de développement brandissent la différence féminine pour justifier la ségrégation et l'abaissement des femmes.

2. Pour une victoire toute symbolique, la mise en place de la parité hommes/femmes dans les assemblées rompt avec ce premier principe de toute émancipation: le refus d'enfermer les êtres dans des distinctions naturelles. Ce faisant, on reconstruit les vieilles barrières entre le monde des femmes et celui des hommes. En voulant donner toute leur place aux femmes, on les laisse à leur place et on renvoie les hommes aux schémas traditionnels qu'ils commençaient à abandonner.

3. En faisant de la « différence » féminine un absolu qui transcende toutes les catégories, on abandonne le principe de la solidarité entre victimes de discriminations. On distingue entre les niveaux d'exclusion, mais on ignore les inégalités économiques, sociales, raciales dont souffrent tant de femmes. Et, en inventant de toutes pièces une solidarité formelle entre les femmes en tant que telles, on oublie trop facilement que toutes les femmes ne sont pas également discriminées.

Venue des femmes, la parité se retournera contre elles, car la ségrégation, qu'elle soit de sexe, de genre, de race entraîne toujours la discrimination. Venue de la gauche, la parité se révélera un obstacle à l'émancipation de tous les autres exclus, figés pour toujours dans une appartenance qui maintient les inégalités.

'Three arguments against parity'

The solution proposed to end the scandalous absence of women from political life is in contradiction with the spirit and principles of progressive politics.

1. It is thought that, to make up for a democratic deficit, we should turn our backs on the universal republic. The universal is a weapon to combat differences in so far as they separate and discriminate. History shows that integration is never achieved in the name of difference but that, conversely, it is always in its name that exclusions occur: see today how developing nations brandish the notion of feminine difference in order to justify the segregation and humiliation of women.

2. In the pursuit of a purely symbolic victory, the implementation of male/female parity in elected assemblies breaks with the first principle of any politics of emancipation: the refusal to confine human beings to natural distinctions. In doing this, old barriers are erected between the world of women and that of men. In wanting to grant women their full place in society, we put them in their place and send men back to the traditional views that they were starting to give up.

3. In making feminine 'difference' an absolute notion that transcends all categories, we give up the principle of solidarity between all victims of discrimination. We distinguish between different levels of exclusion but are not aware of the economic, social and racial inequalities suffered by many women. And, by making up from start to finish the notion of a formal solidarity between women as women, we forget far too easily that all women are not equally discriminated against.

Coming from women, parity will turn against them because segregation, whether it be on the grounds of sex, gender or race, always leads to discrimination. Coming from the Left, parity will turn out to be an obstacle in the emancipation of all the other excluded people in society, fixed forever in a group identity that maintain inequalities.

FURTHER READING

Agacinski, S. 1999. Contre l'effacement des sexes, *Le Monde*, 6 February, p.1.
  Influential article by prominent pro-parity campaigner.
Allwood, G. and Wadia, K. 2000. *Women and politics in France 1958–2000*.
  London: Routledge.
  Insightful analysis of women and political life in France during the Fifth Republic, particularly good on the parity debates.
Badinter, E. 1999. La parité est une régression, *L'Événement*, 744, 4–10
  February.
  Main arguments of prominent anti-parity campaigner.
Cross, M. F. 2000. Women and politics. In Gregory, A. and Tidd, U. (eds)
  Women in contemporary France. Oxford: Berg.
  Concise overview of women and Republican political life, culminating in parity campaign.

10

Conclusion: towards a twenty-first-century Republic

Claire Gorrara and Rachael Langford

On 27 May 2002, France woke up to the biggest electoral shock in the history of the Fifth Republic. In the first round of the presidential elections, the two candidates with the most votes were the incumbent President, **Jacques Chirac** (19.88 per cent), and the Far Right leader, **Jean-Marie Le Pen** (16.86 per cent). The much-predicted scenario of a second round run-off between the President and his Socialist Prime Minister, **Lionel Jospin,** had to be rewritten as Jospin, trailing in third place with 16.18 per cent of the vote, was eliminated. The prospect of choosing between the Centre–Right Chirac and the extremist, Le Pen, was an anathema for left-leaning voters.

In shocked reaction, many leftist voters blamed the pollsters for providing inaccurate information on the popularity of Le Pen and so underplaying the dangers of his election. They had believed that Jospin would easily be propelled into the second round and many had voted for more marginal candidates in the first round, ready to switch to Jospin in a Chirac–Jospin head to head. Others attacked the media for fuelling fears about *insécurité* (law and order), the theme that had been the rallying cry of the Le Pen campaign. People took to the streets to register their protest at the possibility of Le Pen as President, many of them secondary school pupils and university students. Slogans made up and passed among demonstrators illustrated their sense of shock, fear and also disaffection with mainstream politics. 'Votez escroc, pas facho' (Vote for a crook, not a fascist) summed up many people's view that they were left with a choice between a crook (Chirac, implicated in a series of financial scandals) and a fascist sympathizer (Le Pen).

The breakthrough of the Far Right was the result of a combination of factors. First, it seemed that voters were protesting against five years of *cohabitation* when a right-wing President and a left-wing government had governed in tandem. This period of co-existence blurred the distinction between Left and Right, perhaps best illustrated by the neo-liberal economic policies of the leftist coalition government. Unable to see 'clear blue water' between the two, some voters channelled their discontent through their choice of extreme left-wing and right-wing parties. Second, the Le Pen Campaign benefited from the collapse of the vote for candidates representing the Centre–Left governing coalition, *La Gauche Plurielle* (Plural Left). The Left's vote was fragmented between many different candidates with the traditional parties of government scoring very badly. Jospin's score was the poorest showing for a Socialist candidate since 1969, while the Communist candidate, Robert Hue, recorded the worst ever electoral result (3.5 per cent) in the history of the French Communist Party. It seemed that their traditional voters had turned their backs on the Left. Third, Le Pen capitalized on fears about crime and law and order and effectively dictated the terrain on which the campaign would be won. Chirac, in particular, chose to engage with the electorate on similar terms, promising new measures to improve general law and order. Le Pen's trump card was to connect such issues to immigration, the rise of Islam and unemployment. In so doing, he succeeded in appealing to the basic anxieties of a sizable proportion of working-class men and women. The Le Pen vote increased in the industrialized North-East, as well as the strongly Republican South-West. He seemed to speak for a reactionary, populist electorate, fearful of change and the impact of European integration and globalization.

Yet the defeat of the Left and the incursions of the Far Right into mainstream politics also had their roots in a general disaffection with politics. Many commentators noted that voters felt cut off and alienated from politics, particularly in the wake of political scandals, some of which centred on Chirac himself. There was a sense that successive governments, including the Jospin administration, were out of touch with real people, a perception that the demagogue Le Pen used to his advantage. Over 28 per cent of the eligible electorate did not cast their votes, the highest percentage in the history of the Fifth Republic, with the figure rising to 37 per cent among the 18–24 age range. In newspaper article after newspaper article, young French men and women lamented the fact that they had not bothered to vote on 26 April. Indeed, for some commentators, the election result was as much a referendum on the state of the Fifth Republic as anything else. Calling for the 'coming of a Sixth Republic' in the pages of the left-leaning daily *Libération* on 29 April, a group of university academics advocated the wholesale renewal of Republican institutions. They called for individual citizens to participate more directly in democracy via referendums and other electoral mechanisms; for politicians and government figures to be made more publicly accountable; for an equitable and clearly defined distribution of power among the main institutions of the State; and for the role of elected representatives to be renewed. Their final plea was for a 'République des citoyens' (a Republic of citizens).

In the two weeks of campaigning that followed the shock first-round result, popular protest at the Le Pen vote and support for the Republic and liberal democracy culminated in a wave of demonstrations on 1 May. Over one and a half million people took to the streets with placards and banners with nearly half a million people in Paris gathering at the *Place de la République*, a symbolic site of support for the Republic. In calling on people to vote for Chirac on 5 May, many politicians drew on France's historic past and moments of crisis to motivate supporters. Some appealed to the founding values of 1789 and compared Le Pen and his electoral programme to the Vichy regime. Others referred to France's resistance record and its fight for liberation in 1944, while a number drew parallels with the popular protest of May 1968, even if the aims of the mass movements were quite different in ideological terms. In a variety of ways, important flashpoints in French history acted as the spur for individuals and organizations to pronounce their support for the Republic and its values.

On 5 May, Chirac was returned as President with 82 per cent of the vote, compared to 18 per cent for Le Pen. This was the biggest score recorded by a French President but, as Chirac and his campaign team were acutely aware, the landslide was largely due to votes cast by those vehemently opposed to Le Pen and who, in normal circumstances, would have voted for a candidate of the Left. Indeed, Chirac's victory speech made clear that he recognized how much his re-election owed to a generalized sense that the Republic was under threat. He announced that 'la France a reaffirmée son attachement aux valeurs de la République' (France has reaffirmed its commitment to the values of the Republic) in supporting him and underlined his intention to enable the Republic to flourish under his leadership. Indeed, he used the Republican motto of *liberté, égalité, fraternité* to sum up his electoral programme for the next five years:

> La liberté, c'est aussi la reconnaissance du travail et du mérite, la réduction des charges et des impôts. L'égalité, c'est le refus de toute discrimination, ce sont les mêmes droits et les mêmes devoirs pour tous. La fraternité, c'est sauvegarder nos retraites. C'est aider les familles à jouer pleinement leur rôle.

> Freedom also means recognition for work and merit, reducing levies and taxes. Equality means rejecting all forms of discrimination, the same rights and duties for all. Fraternity means safeguarding pensions, helping families to play a full role.

For those on the Left, the only possible interpretation of Chirac's success was as an unequivocal victory for the Republic.

On 9 and 16 June 2002, the French were called to vote again, this time in legislative elections. Some feared that the astounding score for the Far Right in the presidential elections would repeat itself and that this would translate into seats in the French National Assembly. Foreign newspapers, such as *The Guardian*, predicted upsets with the Far Right holding the balance of power in a close-run contest between the Socialists and the newly created Centre–Right coalition, the *Union pour la Majorité Présidentielle* (Union for the Presidential Majority, UMP). In the end, the elections were an overwhelming success for the Centre–Right as they picked up 355 seats and 47.3 per cent of the vote. The Socialist Party came a poor second with 140 seats and 35.55 per cent of the vote. Neither the Front National nor any of the other extreme right- and left-wing parties who had fared so well in the first round of the presidential elections took a seat. It seemed business as usual. Yet, there were some worrying signs. As one commentator noted, a 'third force' was emerging in French politics: abstentionism. Some 35.62 per cent of eligible voters in the first round of the legislative elections did not cast their vote. After the crisis of Le Pen's first round presidential score in April, it seemed that such popular activism had not impacted meaningfully on people's perception of politics in general.

What is the future for the Republic in the twenty-first century? As this book has shown, the model of Republican democracy in France is one that has evolved in response to a series of national and international events. It is a form of government and a set of institutions that has faced threats from both the Right and the Left and still continued to represent the collective will of the French people. It has stood firm against the challenges posed by monarchism, authoritarian leadership and class conflict in the nineteenth century. It has survived the horrors of the First World War, the collaboration of the Vichy government, the consequences of decolonization, the popular protest of May 1968 and, more recently, the constitutional reforms of the parity campaign. Yet, the *électrochoc* of the presidential elections of April/May 2002 points to the continuing presence of troubling issues to do with democracy, participation and citizenship that France shares with a good number of its European neighbours, whether Republican or not. How to engage with disaffected voters; how to communicate and ease the transitions required by the processes of European integration; how to defend and promote national interests in a global economy; how to confront international dilemmas, such as global migration and terrorism in the wake of 11 September 2001? With over two centuries of history behind it, the Republic remains an integral part of French public and private life, but it may yet find that its most testing days are still to come.

Glossary of names

Below is a brief summary of the major figures referred to in the preceding chapters, enabling readers to situate them at a glance.

Agacinski, Sylviane (1946–) University philosophy lecturer at the prestigious École des Hautes Études in Paris. Vocal supporter of the parity campaign during the 1990s.

d'Agoult, Marie (1805–76) A novelist who organized an influential literary salon in 1848 and who was a key figure in the feminist movement of this period. She wrote an important history of the 1848 revolution.

Arago, François (1786–1853) Minister of War in the 1848 Provisional Government. He played a key role in the abolition of slavery in the colonies.

Auroux, Jean (1942–) Minister of Labour 1981–82. Architect of the Auroux Laws (1982) that improved trade union and workers' rights in France. Subsequently Secretary of State for Energy (1983–84) and Transport (1984–85), and Minister for Urbanism (1985–86).

Badinter, Élisabeth (1944–) Cultural historian and philosopher of gender relations and identity, she was highly visible in the media due to her vocal opposition to the parity campaign in the 1990s.

Barbusse, Henri (1873–1935) Front-line soldier and journalist; author of Goncourt prize-winning novel, *Le feu* (1916). Received praise and condemnation for his realistic portrayal of trench conditions and battles.

Barrès, Maurice (1862–1923) Writer and politician, involved first with the Boulangist movement. Barrès' political ideas moved towards a mystical and reactionary nationalism, enshrined in his trilogy of novels *Le roman de l'énergie nationale* (1897–1902). Writer of patriotic articles during the First World War.

Bismarck, Otto von (1815–98) the architect of German unification. A political right-winger from Prussian aristocracy, Bismarck was elected President of the Prussian Parliament in 1847, having forced through the modernization of the Prussian army in the 1860s. German unification was achieved in 1871 following the Franco-Prussian war. Bismarck was the first Chancellor of a unified Germany.

Blanc, Louis (1811–82) A radical Socialist who was head of the Luxemburg Commission which established the National Workshops in 1848. He was suspected of involvement in the June uprising and fled to England, returning only after the fall of the Second Empire.

Blanqui, Auguste (1805–81) A revolutionary Socialist involved in the uprisings of 1830, 1848 and 1871 who advocated armed insurrection to aid political change. He was elected President of the Paris Commune in 1871 while in prison but was not active in the Commune due to his imprisonment.

Blum, Léon (1872–1950) Socialist leader and founder of the newspaper *Le Populaire*, Blum was the first Socialist and Jewish Prime Minister of France under the Popular Front government (1936–37). Advocated resistance to Hitler, arrested by the Vichy regime and unsuccessfully tried and imprisoned. Special ambassador to the USA (1946); served a final term as Prime Minister, from December 1946 to January 1947.

Bonaparte, Louis Napoléon (1769–1821) Born a Corsican, Napoléon attended military school and graduated as an officer. The Revolutionary wars favoured his quick promotion and he was made a General at 24. After his *coup d'état* in 1799, he became Emperor in 1804. Died in exile in 1821; his ashes were transported to Paris in 1840.

Boulanger, General Georges (1837–91) Professional soldier, Minister of War in 1886, elected deputy for Paris in 1899 and leader of the anti-Republican Boulangist movement. Advocated extreme nationalism and war-mongering with Germany. Failed to capitalize on popular support in order to mount a *coup d'état* in 1899. Tried for treason in exile; committed suicide in 1891.

Briand, Aristide (1862–1932) Leftist deputy and Prime Minister (1916–17, 1920–21). As Minister of Foreign Affairs (1925–32), advocated reconciliation with Germany through the Locarno Treaties and the Kellogg-Briand Pact. Also designed a plan for a 'United States of Europe', recognized as a forerunner to the European Union. Nobel Peace Prize winner in 1926.

Brion, Hélène (1882–1962) Feminist and socialist nursery schoolteacher prosecuted by Clemenceau's (q.v.) government for distributing anti-war pamphlets in 1917. Received support from political and literary luminaries. Though convicted, Brion did not serve time in jail.

Caillaux, Joseph (1893–1944) Radical Party Prime Minister (1911–12) and deputy. Prosecuted by Clemenceau's (q.v.) wartime government in 1917 for treasonous activities but acquitted.

Carnot, Hippolyte (1801–88) Education Minister in the 1848 Provisional Government. He remained a deputy during the Second Empire, but was not allowed to take his seat since he refused to pledge allegiance to the Emperor.

Cavaignac, General Louis Eugène (1802–57) In 1848, he was recalled to Paris from his posting as Governor General of Algeria to put down the June revolution. Subsequently became head of government but was defeated by Louis-Napoléon in the 1848 presidential elections.

Césaire, Aimé (1913–) Martinique poet, playwright and politician; co-founder of the *négritude* movement; fierce critic of European colonialism and hypocrisy (*Cahier d'un retour au pays natal*, 1935; *Discours sur le colonialisme*, 1955).

Charles X (1757–1836) Younger brother of Louis XVI (q.v.) and Louis XVIII (q.v.), reigning monarch in France 1824–30. Right-wing and extremely hostile to the Revolution and democratic politics, Charles succeeded to the throne on the death of Louis XVIII. His undemocratic politics led to his downfall in the July Revolution of 1830. He then lived in exile in Prague until his death.

Chirac, Jacques (1932–) Gaullist politician and leader of the RPR (*Rassemblement du Peuple Français*, 'Grouping of the French People') for many years. He was mayor of Paris and has served as Prime Minister on two occasions: 1974–76 and 1986–88. Elected as President of the Republic in 1995, he was returned to office for a second term in April 2002.

Clemenceau, Georges (1841–1929) Doctor, journalist and Republican statesman. Nicknamed 'The Tiger', he was Radical Party Prime Minister in 1906–9 and 1917–20. Suppressed dissent as premier in 1917. Played a key role in the post-First World War Versailles Treaty; campaigned for harsh reparations from Germany.

Cohn-Bendit, Daniel (1945–) Spokesman for the M22M movement and main leader of the May 1968 student movement. Now an MEP for the French Green Party.

Couve de Murville, Maurice (1907–99) French diplomat and politician. Minister for Foreign Affairs, 1958–68; Prime Minister from July 1968 until July 1969 when he stepped down following the resignation of President de Gaulle (q.v.).

Cresson, Édith (1934–) The first (and to date only) woman to have served as French Prime Minister (1991–92). Appointed by Socialist President François Mitterrand (q.v.), her term in office was short and unpopular. Since then she has acted as an EU Commissioner (1994–2000).

Daladier, Édouard (1884–1970) Radical deputy and Prime Minister (1934 and 1938–40). Resigned from office following attempted *coup d'état* of 1934. As premier in 1938, presided with Neville Chamberlain over the Munich Agreement that ceded a portion of Czechoslovakia to the Germans.

Danton, Georges Jacques (1759–94) A French Revolutionary activist, Danton became an ardent member of the Jacobin club in 1792 and, soon after, a controlling member of the Committee of Public Safety. He was replaced by Robespierre (q.v.) in 1793 and guillotined in 1794.

Doriot, Jacques (1898–1945) Leader of a French fascist party, the *Parti Populaire Français* (French Popular Party) during the Second World War, Doriot was an virulent anti-Communist and exponent of close ideological ties with Nazi Germany. He was killed in 1945 while in exile in Germany.

Dreyfus, Captain Alfred (1859–1935) A Jewish army captain tried, in 1899, for passing confidential documents to the Germans. Dreyfus maintained his innocence but was sentenced to hard labour on Devil's Island. The campaign for his retrial split France into violently opposed camps. In July 1906, a retrial cleared Dreyfus. He was reinstated to the army, awarded the Legion of Honour and served during the First World War.

Drieu la Rochelle, Pierre (1893–1945) Fascist literary figure who also wrote popular novels condemning France's decadence during the inter-war period. During the wartime Vichy regime, he was an ardent defender of collaboration and eventually committed suicide rather than face trial.

Drumont, Édouard (1844–1917) Journalist who wrote the anti-Semitic *La France juive* (1886). From 1892, founded and edited the virulent anti-Dreyfus (q.v.), anti-Semitic newspaper, *La Libre Parole*.

Ferry, Jules François Camille (1832–93) Republican politician. Twice Prime Minister and once Minister of Foreign Affairs during the Third Republic. Known mainly for the Ferry Laws (1882), establishing free, compulsory, secular primary education, and for extending the French colonial empire. Attacked in 1893, he died from his injuries.

Frenay, Henri (1905–88) Ex-army officer, who co-founded the Resistance group *Combat* during the Second World War. He was closely involved in preparation for the liberation of France in 1944 and was appointed Minister for Deportees, Prisoners of War and Refugees in the post-war government.

Garnier-Pagès, Louis (1803–78) Participated actively in the banquets organized against Louis-Philippe's (q.v.) constitutional monarchy, and became Minister of Finance in the Provisional Government of 1848.

de Gaulle, Charles (1890–1970) French general and statesman. French Resistance leader during the Second World War; host of the 1944 Brazzaville Conference; politician responsible for granting independence to Sub-Saharan and North Africa; architect and first President of the Fifth Republic, 1959–69.

Gide, André (1869–1951) Major French novelist, playwright and essayist; winner of the Nobel Prize for Literature in 1947; critic of French colonialism (*Voyage au Congo*, 1927; *Retour du Tchad*, 1928) and co-sponsor of the journal *Présence Africaine*.

de Gouges, Olympe (1755–93) During the French Revolution, she spoke out against the bloodshed of the Terror and was guillotined in 1793 as a reactionary royalist. Her fame comes from her drafting of the 'Declaration of the Rights of Woman and the Citizeness' where she claimed equality for women with men in all aspects of public and private life.

Guizot, François (1787–1874) Foreign Minister and head of government under Louis-Philippe (q.v.). His conservative policies favoured the propertied and moneyed classes and his refusal to consider reform created the popular dissatisfaction that sparked the 1848 revolution.

Jaurès, Jean (1859–1914) Leader of the French Socialists, and founder of the newspaper *L'Humanité*. He unified factions of the Left into a single socialist party, the *Section Française de l'Internationale Ouvrière* (French Section of the International Workers' Movement). Assassinated by an ultra-nationalist extremist on 31 July 1914.

Joffre, Joseph (1852–1931) First Commander-in-chief of the French army during the First World War. Received praise for his defence of Paris at the Battle of the Marne in the opening weeks of the war.

Jospin, Lionel (1937–) A Socialist politician and university lecturer by profession, Jospin served as a Minister for Education, 1988–92. He was appointed as Prime Minister in 1997 and stood for a second time as the Socialist candidate for President in 2002. Beaten to the second round by Jean Marie Le Pen (q.v.), he has declared his intention to retire from politics.

La Fayette, Gilbert du Motier, Marquis de (1757–1834) A Major General during the American Civil War, Lafayette returned triumphant to the French court in 1783. Despite his drafting of the 'Declaration of the Rights of Man and the Citizen', the tide of the Revolution turned against him and he escaped abroad.

Lamartine, Alphonse de (1790–1869) A poet whose political career reached its zenith in 1848 when he became Foreign Minister and head of the Provisional Government. He withdrew from politics during the Second Empire, but remained opposed to Louis-Napoléon's regime.

La Rocque, Colonel François de (1885–1946) Leader of the *Croix de Feu* (Cross of Fire), the largest inter-war fascist political movement. Transformed the movement into the *Parti Social Français* (French Social Party) in 1936. Initially supported the wartime Vichy regime but later joined the Resistance.

Laval, Pierre (1883–1945) Five times Foreign Minister and four times Premier before 1939, Laval was twice head of the Vichy regime during the Second World War. Not an ideological fascist, he justified cooperation with Nazi Germany as in France's best interests. He was tried and executed for treason in 1945.

Ledru-Rollin, Alexandre (1807–74) Founder of the newspaper *La Réforme*, and Interior Minister in the 1848 Provisional Government. He spearheaded the introduction of universal male suffrage. Involved in a counter-revolution to Louis-Napoléon's regime in June 1849, he fled to London, returning to France only in 1870.

Léon, Pauline (1758–?) The daughter of a Paris chocolate maker, she welcomed the Revolution with enthusiasm and joined the Jacobins in 1791, addressing the National Assembly on behalf of Parisian women. Léon was one of the founders of the Society of Republican Revolutionary Women and became its President in 1793. Critical of the Terror, in 1794 she and her husband were arrested and imprisoned.

Le Pen, Jean-Marie (1928–) Leading French Far Right politician; soldier in the Indo-Chinese and Algerian Wars; founder and leader of the racist extreme right-wing French political party, the *Front National* (National Front) (1972); candidate in four Presidential elections, taking second place to Jacques Chirac (q.v.) in 2002.

Louis XVI (1754–93) King at 20, Louis was little prepared to govern as his brother, who died young, had been expected to reign. He was overcome by the events of the Revolution and guillotined in 1793.

Louis XVII (1785–95) Titular king of France from 1793 to 1795. He died in prison.

Louis XVIII (1755–1824) King of France from 1814 to 1824. Younger brother of Louis XVI and older brother of Charles X (q.v.). He was restored to the throne in 1814 after the defeat of Napoléon I. He abdicated on Napoléon's return and was restored to the throne again in 1815. Politically moderate at first, his reign became reactionary as it continued.

Louis-Napoléon, Napoléon III (1808–73) Nephew of Napoleon Bonaparte (q.v.), spent much of his early life in exile. He returned to France in 1848 when he was elected to the Assembly, and subsequently to the Presidency. He seized power in a *coup d'état* in 1851 and proclaimed the Second Empire in December 1852. His reign was brought to an end by the French defeat in the Franco-Prussian war (1870–71).

Louis-Philippe (1773–1850) King of France 1830–48. He was brought to power by the middle classes after the 1830 revolution, as a representative of order. After the 1848 revolution he exiled himself in London.

MacMahon, Marshal Marie Edme Patrice de (1808–93) Professional soldier and politician of reactionary, monarchist views. Army commander during the Franco-Prussian war (1870–71); aided the repression of the Paris Commune (1871). President of the Third Republic (1873–79); instigated a constitutional crisis in 1877 by dissolving the Republican government and trying to replace it with a monarchist government.

Marat, Jean-Paul (1743–93) An outspoken journalist during the French Revolution, Marat was extremely hostile to the nobility and the King. He was murdered in his bath by Charlotte Corday in 1793.

Marie-Antoinette, de Hapsbourg-Lorraine (1755–93) The fourth daughter of Empress Marie-Thérèse of Austria, she married the French Dauphin who became Louis XVI (q.v.). She was known for a lavish lifestyle and was guillotined during the Revolution in 1793, aged 38, soon after her husband.

Marx, Karl (1818–83) Influential German political and economic historian and analyst. Marx considered France to be a model for modern political development, and he wrote important theoretical analyses of the events in France of 1848–51 and 1870–71.

Massu, Jacques (1908–) General, known primarily for his military role during the Algerian war of independence (1954–62). Led French troops during the Battle of Algiers (1957) and was military commander of Algiers (1958–60).

Mauriac, François (1885–1970) Major French Catholic novelist of the twentieth century; right-wing critic of France's practice of torture in the Algerian War; co-founder of the weekly journal *L'Express*.

Maurras, Charles (1862–1952) Polemicist, poet and essayist. Leading member of the *Action Française* (French Action) group, and editor of extreme monarchist newspaper *L'Action Française* (1908–44). Arrested in 1944 for collaboration. Tried and condemned to penal servitude for life, but freed in 1952 on health grounds and died shortly after.

Mendès France, Pierre (1907–82) Became a Radical deputy in 1932 and member of the second Popular Front cabinet in 1938. Served in Fourth Republic governments, including as President of the Council of Ministers (Prime Minister) in 1954–55. Hostile to the Fifth Republic Constitution, he joined the *Parti Socialiste Unifié* (Unified Socialist Party, PSU) in 1961.

Michel, (Clémence-) Louise (1830–1905) Schoolteacher and Republican activist under the Second Empire and a political speaker during the Commune. Deported to New Caledonia for her part in the uprising, she returned only in 1880. Subsequently became a popular touring speaker advocating anarchist/anti-authoritarian politics.

Mitterrand, François (1916–96) French statesman. Often a minister in Fourth Republic governments. With the advent of the Fifth Republic, he united the Left and built up the Socialist Party after becoming its leader in 1971. Became President in 1981, and was the first to win a second term of office, 1988–95.

Moulin, Jean (1899–1943) French regional administer for the Eure-et-Loire, Moulin rallied to the Resistance and acted as General de Gaulle's (q.v.) envoy to the internal resistance movements in France during the Second World War. Captured and tortured to death in 1943.

Muller, Annette (1933–) Born into an immigrant Polish family, Muller was one of many thousands of Jewish children living in France rounded up for deportation to the death camps during the Second World War. She escaped their fate and testifies to her experiences in *La petite fille du Vél d'Hiv* (1991).

Nivelle, General Robert (1856–1924) Gained notoriety for his unit's performance at Verdun during the First World War. Replaced Joffre (q.v.) as Commander-in-chief in 1916. Known for the disastrous 1917 offensive which led to a series of mutinies in the French ranks.

Papon, Maurice (1910–) Secretary-general of Vichy's regional administration for the Bordeaux region during the Second World War, 1942–44. Over 50 years later in April 1998, Papon was convicted for complicity in crimes against humanity for his part in the deportation of Jews from France to the death camps during the war period.

Pétain, Henri-Philippe (1856–1951) A distinguished First World War military leader, Pétain was elected head of the collaborating Vichy government during the Second World War and instituted a series of reactionary policies, known as the National Revolution. Tried and convicted for treason after the Liberation.

Pompidou, Georges (1911–74) Fifth Republic statesman; Prime Minister under de Gaulle (q.v.), 1962–68, but stepped down following the May 1968 crisis. President from 1969 until his death in 1974.

Proudhon, Pierre-Joseph (1809–65) Anarchist/Socialist philosopher, writer and activist, influenced by Karl Marx (q.v.). Elected to the Constituent Assembly of 1848, Proudhon held radical views on the just organization of society. His followers were active members of the First International of 1864, and his ideas were a dominant influence on French Socialist thought at a time when Marx's work was relatively unknown.

Robespierre, Maximilien de (1758–94) Trained as a lawyer, Robespierre was sympathetic to extreme left-wing ideas and became a Jacobin. In 1793, he took over leadership of the Committee of Public Safety from Danton (q.v.). He was subsequently arrested and finally guillotined in 1794 along with many of his supporters.

Roudy, Yvette (1929–) A Socialist politician and supporter of François Mitterrand (q.v.), Roudy was appointed as the first Minister for Women's Rights (1981–86). One of her biggest achievements in office was the 1983 *loi Roudy* on equality at work.

Sand, George (1804–76) A novelist and activist whose political stances were strongly influenced by her feminist convictions and utopian socialist beliefs. She was an aide to Ledru-Rollin (q.v.) under the Provisional Government of 1848, and wrote for the *Bulletin de la République*. Disappointed by the events of June 1848, she withdrew from political life.

Sartre, Jean-Paul (1905–80) Leading French philosopher, novelist and playwright; an existentialist and long-time Marxist; co-editor of the intellectual journal, *Les Temps Modernes*; vociferous opponent of France's wars of decolonization in Indo-China (1946–54) and Algeria (1954–62).

Séguy, Georges (1927–) Communist trade union activist. Secretary-General of the *Confédération Générale du Travail* (General Confederation of Labour, CGT), 1967–82 and member of the *Parti Communiste Français* (French Communist Party, PCF) since 1942, including of its Central Committee since 1954 and its politbureau (1956–82).

Senghor, Léopold Sédar (1906–2001) Prominent African intellectual and poet; Senegal's first President (1960–80); an ardent critic of the French Republican doctrine of *assimilation* of indigenous peoples and their cultures.

Thiers, Adolphe (1797–1877) Historian, politician and statesman. A supporter of the 1830 Revolution and twice Prime Minister under the July Monarchy, Thiers was an avowed opponent of Louis-Napoléon (q.v.). As the first President of the Third Republic, he was intransigent in crushing the Paris Commune.

Veil, Simone (1927–) As a Gaullist politician and Health Minister, Veil introduced a law to legalize abortion in the face of fierce opposition in 1974. The *loi Veil* became law provisionally in 1975 and was confirmed in 1979.

Waldeck Rousseau, René (1864–1904) Statesman of the moderate Republican Left, twice Minister of the Interior, and Prime Minister 1899–1902. Responsible for the Waldeck Rousseau law of 1884 legalizing trade unions. He succeeded in securing a presidential pardon for Alfred Dreyfus (q.v.).

Zola, Émile (1840–1902) Prolific novelist (author of the 20-volume *Rougon-Macquart* cycle of novels), and politically moderate intellectual. Zola was both a man of letters and a renowned public figure. His famous intervention in the Dreyfus (q.v.) affair, 'J'accuse' (1898), led to fines and imprisonment. Some have suggested that his death in suspicious circumstances may have been due to right-wing enemies.

Time chart

Below is a brief chronology of some key dates in France since the Revolution, to help situate the historical discussion in the book chapters at a glance.

FRENCH REVOLUTION (1789–1799)

1789   Meeting of the Estates General; storming of the Bastille; drafting of the 'Declaration of the Rights of Man and the Citizen'

1792   War declared against Austria and Prussia. Fall of the monarchy

FIRST REPUBLIC (1792–1804)

1793   Execution of Louis XVI

1793–1794   The Terror

1795–1799   The Directorate

1799–1804   The Consulate: Napoléon Bonaparte as First Consul, then Emperor

FIRST EMPIRE (1804–1814)

1814   Napoléon abdicates

BOURBON RESTORATION (1814–1830)

1814–1824   Reign of Louis XVIII

1824–1830   Reign of Charles X

1830   July Revolution and crowning of Louis-Philippe

ORLÉANS MONARCHY (1830–1848)

Reign of Louis-Philippe

SECOND REPUBLIC (1848–1852)

1848   Revolutions of February and June; Louis-Napoléon elected President

1851   *Coup d'état* of Louis-Napoléon

SECOND EMPIRE (1852–1870)

1852   Louis-Napoléon proclaimed Emperor (Napoléon III)

1870–1871   Franco-Prussian War; fall of Napoléon III

THIRD REPUBLIC (1879–1940)

1871	Paris Commune
1875	Republican constitution established
1885–1889	Boulanger affair
1894–1906	Dreyfus affair
1905	Separation of Church and State
1914–1918	First World War
1919	Versailles Treaty
1933	Hitler comes to power in Germany
1936–1937	Victory of the Popular Front under Léon Blum
1939	France declares war on Germany
1940	Defeat of France; German occupation of northern France; dissolution of Third Republic

VICHY REGIME (1940–1944)

1940	Pétain comes to power; de Gaulle's 18 June appeal to Resistance
1942	Round-up of Jews in Paris; German occupation of southern France
1944	Brazzaville Conference; Liberation of France; purges of collaborators

PROVISIONAL GOVERNMENT OF DE GAULLE (1945–46)

1945	Women vote for the first time in French elections

FOURTH REPUBLIC (1946–1958)

1946–1954	Indo-Chinese war of liberation
1954–1962	Algerian war of independence
1958	Insurrection in Algeria; de Gaulle assumes power in France

FIFTH REPUBLIC (1958–)

1959	De Gaulle elected President
1968	Events of May 1968
1969	Resignation of de Gaulle; Pompidou becomes President
1974	Giscard d'Estaing elected President
1981	François Mitterrand elected President
1986–1988	'Cohabitation' of Socialist President and right-wing government
1988	Mitterrand wins a second term as President
1995	Jacques Chirac elected President
1997–2002	'Cohabitation' of Centre–Right President and left-wing government
1999	Parity campaign succeeds in changing French Constitution
2002	Jacques Chirac wins second term as President; parties of the Right win legislative elections

Index